A Journey to Purpo
and First Respo

SERVICE

AND

SOUL

Jenna Griffith

Service and Soul:
A Journey to Purpose for Military and First Responder Wives

Copyright © 2023 Jenna Griffith

Published by Made to Change the World™ Publishing
Nashville, Tennessee

Cover and interior design by Chelsea Jewell

ISBN: 978-1-956837-26-1 Hardcover
         978-1-956837-27-8 eBook

Printed in the USA, Canada, Australia, and Europe

To the women who are holding down the fort
and wearing all the hats at home.
To the women who feel like they are missing out on their purpose.
To the women who don't feel like they're enough to have it all.
To all the women fighting an unseen battle.
This book is dedicated to you.

I see you.
I hear you.
I am you.

There is space in this world for you!
May you find in these pages the tools and strategies to harness the
strength within you and live the life of your dreams.

CONTENTS

ACKNOWLEDGMENTS

It truly does take a village to make this dream to write a book come true. Without these supportive, inspirational, and loving people in my life, I wouldn't have given this gift to myself and all who will read it.

First, I would like to thank my heavenly Father. I have witnessed His love and promises in the many phases of my life. Throughout the writing of this book, I was reminded of all the times that He gave me hope and strength to carry on. Without Him, I would not have known what true faith can do.

They say you should marry someone who wants to chase your dreams with you, and that I did. I owe so much of my perseverance to my husband, Seth. Thank you for always helping me believe that I can accomplish and succeed at anything I desire. Your love and encouragement throughout this process have pulled me through when I wanted to give up. Thank you for holding me accountable and constantly encouraging me to be a better version of myself. You make me believe that I can do anything in this world!

Without my children, I wouldn't have many of these stories. Camden and Zachary, I love being your mom! Without the two of you, I truly wouldn't feel whole. Camden, you changed my life and made me a mom for the first time, and, even though you didn't know it, you helped me understand what true unconditional love feels like. You were and always will be my gift, Camden. And, sweet Zachary, the miracle of your existence is one that is hard to even put into words. You taught me how to let go of control and trust that God would provide and redeem. I'm so proud and grateful to have you both as my children! Kyle and Caitlin, my bonus children, thank you for taking me in and letting me love you. I'm honored to be even a couple of chapters in your amazing stories. May you all learn from my example that every single dream is worth seeing through if it's important to you!

To my mom, thank you for being such a faithful supporter of me through all of this. I'm forever grateful for your guidance to be a woman of God. Thank you for always being just one phone call away for prayer, love, and advice. I am so grateful to have such a powerhouse of a woman teaching me how to be the same. I love you dearly and hope this makes you proud!

If you're lucky enough to have one ride-or-die best friend, you have everything you could ever need. My life will forever be brighter with my best friend, Anita, by my side. You have bravely held my hand through it all—loving me, supporting me, and strengthening me. You have taught me how to stand tall even when I didn't want to, and I will forever be grateful for that. Thank you for always showing up and always being my greatest cheerleader and confidant!

A special thanks to Tiffany Peterson. You were the one who opened my eyes to the healing world and the journey of loving myself. Thank you for leading the way for so many who are longing for purpose and true joy in life.

Thank you to Ellie Shefi, my writing coach and publisher. Thank you for creating space for me to share my message and for encouraging me to write this book so I can help other women who are where I once was.

To my family and the many other amazing people in my life who have helped shape me into who I am today, I am eternally grateful.

INTRODUCTION

Writing a book has been a vision of mine for a long time. Everything in my life that has led to this moment was created to be shared to help others. I was used and tried in those times to become a future example and support to other women going through similar situations.

I almost didn't write this book. Someone close to me challenged my authority and ability to write a book that could help other people. I let that one person's opinion derail my book mission for nearly eight years despite countless others telling me that my story needed to be told. I am sure you can relate.

My journey has been full of twists and turns. From being a mother at eighteen, to marrying a soldier who struggled with trauma and addiction, to having a premature child born who would then struggle with autism, to starting a thriving business in my late thirties when most would think it was too late.

And yet ...

Through it all, here I am.

I know my story is not unique. I know so many of you have also faced challenges that have left you feeling unseen, unheard, and unworthy. But that stops now.

It's time for me to tell my story.

Like so many of you, I've had fears, doubts, and imposter syndrome. No one, including me, ever thought that I would write a book. I had every reason in the world to walk away from completing it. I could have made excuse after excuse as to why I didn't have time, how I wasn't qualified enough, or how no one would read it. Who even cares about what I have to say? You do. That's why you're here, right?

You want to know that you have a purpose. You want to know that your existence is more than being a wife, a mother, or an employee punching a clock. You desperately want to get off the hamster wheel and find joy, laughter, and fulfillment. I've got you, sister! You don't have to settle for being caged, playing small, being silenced, or dimming your light any longer!

You want more for your life. You know there are strategies that you can use to get what you want. And you're right! Within the pages of this book, I will share those strategies with you. After all, this book was created for you!

CHAPTER 1
From There to Here

It's 8:30 on a Friday night, and I collapse into my bed in a full-blown bawling session. You know, the kind of crying where you can barely catch your breath and you've got snot everywhere. What Oprah calls the "ugly cry." I had just moved into my new townhome and was going through a divorce. I had two small children, a job that I had practically begged for, and no real idea how I was going to pay my bills. I remember laying there thinking, "This has to be the lowest low with the highest feeling of gratitude that I have ever felt in my life."

Let me explain.

I was going through a very uncomfortable, challenging, extraordinary life experience, yet I felt incredibly free, liberated, and excited for my future. Even though I didn't know what the next step was, I knew that I was making the right decision for me and my family. Have you ever felt that way? Like you made a decision that you had been putting off for a long time, and, when you finally made it, you felt like you were flying? I knew that day was a turning point for me for so many different reasons. I had consciously made a choice to walk through my fear with courage I didn't even know I had at the time.

I had spent the last ten years of my life as a military wife. That's *who* I was. That was my identity. Or at least that's what I thought. I was the one standing back so that my then-husband could bravely go and fight for our freedom. It was my duty to take care of the house, take care of the children, and, most importantly, not complain about it. Looking back, I realize that's why most of the military wives that I met, especially those whose marriages ended in divorce, felt like they were robbed of years of their lives. We were taught that we were the "silent soldiers." We were the ones who held down the fort while our men were gone, and we did it with a smile and without requesting anything that could be deemed selfish. I'm, of course, grateful for our soldiers and their sacrifice for our freedom. I'm now married to a beautiful man who served twenty years in the Air Force and currently works to save lives all over the world. But, with that, I am also grateful for the amazing spouses who often get passed over and underappreciated.

That night, lying and crying in my bed, I knew that I was about to step into the life that I had been dreaming of for ten years. I knew that I was made for more, but I didn't know what that *more* looked like. I was courageously curious yet, simultaneously, full of doubt about my future. I held the limiting belief that, at thirty-one years old and a single mother with no clue what I wanted to do with my life, I was way too late to the game. Questions flooded my mind:

› Is it too late?
› Do I have what it takes?
› What skills do I have?
› What authority do I have?
› Do I need to go back to school?

I asked myself all these questions while trying not to freak out about my situation. So I learned, in those moments, to ask the questions *and* lean into the answers with curiosity. I would quietly listen for the answers, and, eventually, they would come.

You might be wondering what led to that point in my life—that night I ugly-cried on my bed—that night where I realized I was finally ready to step into the woman I was meant to be. It started when I became a teen mom. I was fresh out of high school and decided that I was going to flee the nest in Tennessee and follow my best friend to good ol' Hotlanta (slang for Atlanta back in the day). Back then, I was invincible with a whole life ahead of me. I was going to move down there, party with my friends while working a job as a waitress, and, most importantly, make my own rules! I had it all figured out, until I didn't. In just a short three months, all of that changed. I was pregnant and barely eighteen years old. Oh, and did I mention that I was raised in a strict southern Christian family? Yeah, you can imagine how terrified I was to break that news to my family. Luckily for me, they stepped up to help me raise that sweet first-born angel, who is now twenty years old. Was I still scared? Heck yes! But I also learned so much from it. I had to grow up fast, really fast. I no longer only had to worry about me and my own well-being. If you relate to this story, then you know the feeling of pressure from that sort of responsibility while all of your friends are seemingly out living a dream life.

I was married at the age of twenty-two to a soldier in the U.S. Army, and our first duty station was in Fort Carson, Colorado. The military makes it easy to jump right into a marriage with its steady paychecks, free insurance, and extra pay to be married. Not only had I fallen in love, but he fell in love with me *and* my son. He accepted us as a package deal and was able to provide for us. I didn't fully commit to my life in Colorado because I missed my family in Tennessee so much. But I quickly became pregnant with our first child together because that was the "next step" in this new life. At thirteen weeks gestation, I was t-boned at an intersection and lost that child. This was the first time that I experienced the lack of community within the military. My husband was away at training, and my extended family was in Tennessee. I was told that the FRG (Family Readiness Group) would take care of me. I didn't even know who the FRG was or why I had to lean on them for support. I didn't understand why my husband couldn't come home and be with me! He was grieving too!

But "that's the way it is," I was told. I quickly learned that I was on my own to figure things out when he was gone. Most importantly, I learned that I didn't just fall in love with a man who happened to be a soldier, I signed up to serve too. I signed up to accept the mission no matter what was going on in our lives. I signed up to not ask questions or ask why. I signed up to pick up the pieces of the home and the children while he was gone, as well as the pieces of him that came back. That was my job.

We soon moved from Fort Carson to Fort Bragg, North Carolina, so my husband could go through a special operations medical training school. Just three months after losing our last child, I became pregnant again. We were only supposed to be in Fort Bragg for six months, but, unfortunately, I went into labor at just twenty-three weeks gestation. Our son was barely able to survive due to his low birth weight and brain bleeding. We were told by four different doctors that he would have no quality of life and that we needed to let him go. After 127 NICU days, 15 shunt surgeries, and 2 rounds of viral meningitis, we had a semi-healthy little boy at home. That was a pivotal turning point in both of our lives because we knew that we would have to take extra care of him. Since then, he has needed three more surgeries and has been diagnosed with autism and ADHD. We had every reason to feel sad, hurt, angry, and confused, and ask God "why." But I remember thinking that God would have a purpose in all of that, and He has.

Once we got settled in life, or what felt like settled, we had another major event knock us off our feet. Just a short year after bringing our son home, my husband suffered a TBI (traumatic brain injury) from a hard helicopter landing in Afghanistan. As a military wife, you always have it in the back of your head that you could get *the call.* "Your husband has been in an accident." I instantly fell to my knees and dropped the phone in shock and fear. Luckily, I was with a good friend who was there to pick up the phone and support me. I can't even fathom what it would've been like to hear that he wasn't coming home at all.

He made it back to the states within the week, and, before we knew it, we were temporarily living in a hotel in Omaha, Nebraska, so that he could receive treatment for his brain injury. This is when things started to turn. Unfortunately, and this is a common complaint among military families, when it comes to any sort of recovery from war, the military tries to put a band-aid on a deep wound by prescribing pills. Pills that end up causing numbness and dissociation, and wreck soldiers and their families. This was the start of my then-husband's battle with addiction to pills and alcohol. It would eventually break us both individually and as a married couple.

This is the *CliffsNotes* version of ten years of my life, and maybe I'll write more books one day to really share the full powerful stories. But I want to show that, like you, I have felt like giving up. I have had real, devastating things happen that made me want to go into a deep hole of depression and victimhood. But I knew that those moments were building me up for a bigger life than I understood at the time. The most important thing when you go through trials is to not let them take you down for too long. You have a choice in these moments to either find the lesson or let them *completely derail you from what you were put on Earth to do.* It's scary, I know, but there are ways that you can rise above during those times.

Now take a deep breath and acknowledge your feelings. It's okay to be scared, but don't let that fear hold you back. Change is a natural part of life, and it can be an exciting opportunity for growth and self-discovery. Get in touch with your subconscious mind, the part that influences your thoughts, feelings, and behaviors. You can do this by meditating, journaling, or just taking some quiet time to set an intention for this growth period in your life. Doing this will allow you to focus on aligning your body with your goals by taking care of yourself physically, emotionally, and spiritually.

So what courageous questions are you seeking answers to?

You've found this book because you *are seeking*, so lean in with curiosity to find what you are searching for. Maybe you don't know right now, and that's okay! You're just getting started. I encourage you to ask yourself this question as you move through the steps in this book.

Before moving on, I want to acknowledge that which needs to be celebrated … You! You are here, you showed up, you made a decision! You're ready to see true lasting change in your life. Have you stopped to celebrate? If not, do it right now! I want you to stand up, throw your arms in the air, and say, "Yes! I did this because I believe in me!" It's going to feel silly at first, but give it a try. To warn you, there will be plenty of other silly things that I will encourage you to do because I have done them, and they work. No one will see you, so be brave!

There you go!

Whenever you make changes in your life, you'll feel nervous or resistant toward them. That's completely normal. But the combination of movement and affirmations is a great way to get your nervous system, your subconscious, and your body in alignment as you prepare to make these changes work for you.

CHAPTER 2
Where Energy Goes, Energy Flows

Be patient with yourself while you grow into self-care. Change takes time and effort, but everything you experience is an opportunity to learn and grow. A gentle way to start this momentum is through the practice of gratitude.

An Attitude of Gratitude

Gratitude is one of the most important practices for affecting change in your life. Psychologists Dr. Robert A. Emmons of the University of California, Davis, and Dr. Michael E. McCullough of the University of Miami gathered three groups of individuals and asked them to write sentences each week on particular topics in an attempt to understand the impact gratitude has on the mind and body. The first group wrote about things for which they were grateful; the second group wrote about things that were not pleasing; and the third group wrote about events that impacted their lives, whether positive or negative. After ten weeks, Emmons and McCullough found that participants in the gratitude-focused group were more optimistic and felt better about their lives. They exercised more, had fewer visits to the doctor, and had an overall positive outlook on life (health.harvard.edu/healthbeat/giving-thanks-can-make-you-happier).

When you practice gratitude, your body releases norepinephrine, serotonin, dopamine, and oxytocin—hormones associated with mood regulation and overall well-being. However, when you lack gratitude, your body releases damaging hormones that are associated with stress: adrenaline and cortisol. By practicing gratitude, you have the power within your body to heal or harm yourself. Practicing gratitude is a powerful, yet simple, first step to changing your mindset.

Next, let's take it up a notch.

The Power of Vibration

When you get curious about your life, your experiences, and what they're meant to teach you, you open up an entirely different energetic vibration. And, by vibration, I'm talking about overall energetic power. You are an energetic being walking around in an energetic world. And you can control where your energy goes.

Let's look at an example. Have you ever wanted a new car? You were really excited at the prospect of owning that car and thought about how it would improve your life, how you would feel driving it, and even how it would surpass your current car. Did you also happen to notice many of those types of vehicles out on the road? This phenomenon is called frequency bias. It basically means that your brain has been primed to focus on something specific, positive or negative. That is how energy works. One of my coaches, Tiffany Peterson, summed it up as, "What you think about, you bring about."

Now I want you to think of something very specific. It could be a penny, a butterfly, or a certain type of flower. Anything that comes to mind. I want you to wake up tomorrow morning and think about that same thing. When you go to bed tomorrow, I want you to think about it again. I want you to spend several moments throughout each day thinking about that exact thing. Over the course of the next week or so, count how many times you see that thing in your day-to-day life. Every time you notice it, write it down in the notes section of your phone. At the end of the week, add up how many times this particular object came to you. It's a really neat exercise that shows the power of focus and the power of placing your energy on the things that you want. Once you understand this on a micro level, you will gain confidence to utilize this tool for the much bigger desires of your heart. This is vibration. I use this term throughout the book to help you refocus on the energy that you put out because, "Where energy goes, energy flows!"

Everything works either in harmony or in chaos depending on the type of energy that it is met with. Think about a time that you interacted with someone who wasn't very pleasant. Did you meet their energy with an embrace or resistance? Did you repel it with a good attitude or meet it with a firm sense of "what the heck!?" If you lead with a mindset and vibration of positivity, you likely repelled it like a shield and peacefully moved on with your day. However, if you tend to dish out what you're served, you probably met a roadblock. You have to get real with yourself about where you are.

Vibration is simply the energy that you're putting out every second of the day from the minute you wake up. What's the first thing you do when you wake up? Be honest. Do you reach for your phone? Do you check your social media and say, "Oh my gosh, why on earth is Jessica hanging out with Jake again after everything he did to her?" If so, the next thing you know, you're triggered and sparking up emotions about a past relationship you experienced with someone who treated you badly. In that moment, you are subconsciously deciding how your vibration is going to meet the day. This is why it is so important that you start each and every day setting the intention of the vibration you want to carry. So as you open your eyes, ask yourself, "Who do I want to show up as today? Who do I want to be for myself and for others?"

Look ahead to the feeling that you want to have by the end of the day when you get into bed. What did you accomplish? How did you treat people? What did you do in order to feel whole and complete by the time you laid down to rest?

It wasn't until I understood vibration that I really started to see change in my life. All of a sudden, I was aware of it through every moment of my day, both good and bad. Once you know it, you can't unknow it; it becomes a part of you. And once you know better, as the saying goes, you do better.

Self-Inventory

"In order to be enlightened we have to bring the dark things to light."
- Author Unknown

One of the first exercises I take clients through is a self-inventory. Before any sort of internal changes can be made, you need to be honest with yourself about the current state of your mental and emotional life. But honesty is uncomfortable. It's one of the most difficult practices in life. It's easier to adopt a victim mindset and make excuses for why you might have certain behaviors or outlooks on life. It's easier to place the blame on the hand you've been dealt instead of taking responsibility for the way your life looks. But an inability to be honest with yourself is the greatest roadblock to improving your life. If you want real, lasting change, it starts here.

When I started my healing journey, I was going through my divorce. I had to take a good long look in the mirror and reflect on the ways in which I had contributed. It was painful. I was hurt, angry, and needed someone to pay. I remember that, as more and more attacks and rumors came to my attention, I felt like I needed to defend myself and that my then-husband needed to "make it right." (Later, I will discuss the part of the feminine that was triggering my defensiveness.) The very last thing I wanted to do was to take a self-inventory on my own culpability.

Although a self-inventory exercise isn't easy, it is simple. Enlist the help of a loved one whom you trust and who makes you feel safe. Trust is important because you are going to ask for deep honesty from them that needs to not be met with resistance from you. It needs to be someone who knows your heart. Have a conversation with them about the ways in which you approach situations. Is it with openness, positivity, and flexibility? Or with resistance, negativity, and rigidity? I'm not suggesting toxic positivity or letting people overstep your boundaries and take advantage of you. I'm saying that you can stand up for what's right in your life and still lead with openness and alignment on your overall journey. Life is simply made up of things you can control and things you can't control, and you need to hone your skills to know the difference.

Controlling Your Controllables

Once you have a clear understanding of the current state of your emotional and mental life, you can focus your energy on growth and moving forward. You'll need to learn how to show up for yourself, become curious about your inner world, and make the mental shift necessary to improve the vibration that you are living out. This can be difficult if you feel as though something was done *to* you *by* someone else who should take responsibility. Although that may be true, the greatest way to detach energetically from someone who has harmed you is to release the need for them to correct their wrong. Freeing yourself from the bondage of this mindset is a crucial step toward empowerment and alignment with your inner self.

To control your controllables means to release that which you cannot control. It's hard! Control has always been a big part of my life. I felt that since the military controlled my family's home life due to my then-husband's job, I would control every other part of our lives. Anything that I could control, I would try to control. I thought that was the only way to have power in my life. When you serve alongside a service member, your life is not really yours (or so it feels like). I was constantly trying to find *my place*. Looking back, it was a lesson in learning what I was actually in control of and what I wasn't. Was I in control of another human being's actions? No. Was I in control of my own actions and healing processes? Absolutely. By stepping back and looking at what your controllables are, you create more ease in your life experience. This allows you to move into your own peaceful life journey.

How did you respond to situations over which you had no control? Could you have focused your attention and energy on what you did have control over at the time?

Writing is a great way to let feelings flow through you and helps you shift your mindset. So here are some questions for you to write and reflect on.

What situations or people trigger my need for control?

What are some things in my life over which I need to release control?

_____

_____

_____

_____

_____

How can I practice surrendering control in small ways every day? What are some simple actions I can take to give up control and trust the process?

_____

_____

_____

_____

Who are some people in my life that I can ask for help and support when I feel like I'm losing control? How can I communicate my needs and boundaries effectively?

_____

_____

_____

Expectations Versus Agreements

Before going any further with this journey, it's important to talk about the expectations versus the agreements that you make with yourself and others. Think about how many times you've been let down by either yourself or someone else because of the expectations that you had of the person or the relationship. You are setting yourself up for disappointment, especially when it comes to other people, because not everyone will be aware of what you expect of them. That's why you have agreements.

Understanding the difference between expectations and agreements will help you attain clarity and avoid unnecessary conflict. Expectations are beliefs or assumptions that you have about how people should act or what they should do. They are typically subconscious and are usually based on personal values, past experiences, or cultural norms. Expectations are often one-sided and are usually not well communicated. They can be unrealistic or unreasonable and can lead to disappointment when they are not met. Does this sound like any of your relationships?

Agreements help combat disappointment because they are mutual understandings that are made internally or between you and another person about what you will, or will not, do. Agreements are very clearly defined and communicated. They create a sense of trust, transparency, and accountability. There is intention behind an agreement, and all parties are aware of what has been agreed upon. It creates clarity and alignment and helps to prevent misunderstanding and conflicts.

How much conflict do you think could've been avoided in your life had you had a conversation about agreements and expectations? Knowing your limits when setting agreements, or boundaries, is essential for healthy relationships, not only with others, but with yourself. Understand what you are comfortable with and what you are not, and communicate those limits clearly to others. There are realistic and unrealistic expectations in a relationship, and setting unrealistic expectations can lead to disappointment and frustration. By being honest and transparent about your boundaries, you will find yourself in relationships that are built on trust and respect. Setting boundaries is not about being inflexible or controlling, but about creating a safe and respectful space where everyone's needs are taken into account.

CHAPTER 3
It's the Will, Not the Skill

Decision

Every single thing in life requires a decision.

Do I marry him or not?
Do I take this job or wait for another one?
Do I want mayonnaise or mustard?

Even not making a decision is a decision. If you struggle with indecisiveness, like I used to, you most likely experience a rollercoaster of emotions. The problem with indecisiveness is that it allows other people's opinions to skew and influence your journey. I recall many times when I called on the opinions of others to make a decision. It was normal for me to get their take on a matter yet still feel like I didn't have a clear answer. Why? Because they all had different opinions on what I should or should not do. Why on Earth did I give my power away to people who were not going to be dealing with the consequences of the decisions that I was making? Why did I need permission from someone else to move forward on something that I desired?

Acceptance.

You want to be accepted, admired, and praised for the good choices that you make. It helps you to feel validated and valued by others. You have a fundamental need for social connection and belonging because it affirms your sense of identity and self-worth. It also helps you feel more confident in your choices and can motivate you to continue pursuing your goals. But what may be good for someone else may not be good for you.

My biggest life-changing decision was getting a divorce. I remember sitting with my then-husband in a psychologist's office talking about a new exercise to help my husband through PTSD and his struggle with addiction. The doctor looked at me and told me that, with this particular exercise, things could get worse before they would get better. When he said that, I suddenly had a feeling of certainty rush over me. I couldn't do worse. I had been doing worse for years! I was done with my marriage. I'd had a similar feeling early on in my marriage, but never felt confident enough to act on it for many different reasons. That moment in the psychologist's office was different because, by then, I had experienced so much pain that I knew it was time to focus on my own healing. I immediately burst into tears right then and there; after a while, I fell silent. When we left the building, my husband said, "Don't worry about me, I'll be okay!" You know what I felt right then? Rage. Solid rage. I shouted at him, "I'm not crying about you! I'm crying about myself! When will I get to be okay?!" I remember that moment—I was done with taking the back seat in my own life. I hadn't been putting on my own oxygen mask (or even looking for it for that matter) in over three years! All of the selfless service to others had done nothing but make me bitter toward everyone who didn't appreciate me, including my husband.

Without even questioning it, I made the decision. I knew in my heart that I was finally in a place where I could walk away knowing that I had done every single thing in my power to make the marriage work.

I had clarity about what I could and could not control. Was that decision easy? Absolutely not. I made that decision without having any sort of plan as to what my future would look like. But the decision felt right to me, and everything else would be figured out.

The first step to making any change in your life is to make a decision. Let's unpack what that looks like.

Write out an area of your life where you currently need to make a decision.

_____

_____

_____

_____

_____

_____

Now write out all of your possible options.

_____

_____

_____

_____

_____

Take this a step further and write out the pros and cons of the options. Don't be surprised if your limiting beliefs arise. That's normal. When that happens, identify them. Challenge them by finding evidence that contradicts the beliefs and focusing on more positive and empowering thoughts to reframe them. Practice self-compassion and remind yourself that everyone has doubts and fears and that it's okay to make mistakes and face setbacks.

What comes next is very important. Which option makes you feel most alive? Push through the fear that's fighting to control you. Acknowledge it, but don't give it all the power. Think about which of the above options makes you feel the most peaceful. Write out your preferred option. What do you believe about the outcome of your preferred option?

What is your second-choice option? What do you believe about it?

_____

_____

_____

_____

_____

The best way to work on your decision-making is to start with smaller decisions first. When your husband or friend asks you what you want for dinner, stop responding with the typical, "Whatever you're in the mood for." Start using your voice to claim what you want and trust that you are capable of making good decisions. Decide today that you will listen to your body when making decisions for yourself. Decide today that you will honor yourself above everyone else when making a decision that directly affects you. Make an agreement with yourself, and make it happen!

Commitment

Once you make your decision, commit to seeing it through. The most powerful commitment you can make is to yourself. To hold yourself accountable to your agreements, write out the commitment as a promise to yourself.

I _____ promise to

_____

I make this commitment to myself because I am worthy of a good life, and I deserve it. I make this commitment to myself because it is important to my future self. If I break this commitment, the world will miss out on my light, and I will not be living to my fullest purpose.

Once you've made the commitment to your current and future self, you can step into your ally in this process—the feminine power. Your feminine power is the unique qualities and strengths that you hold within yourself, such as empathy, compassion, intuition, nurturing, and emotional intelligence. Once you learn how to connect to your feminine power, you'll find that you have a stronger sense of self-awareness, confidence, and creativity that will lead to greater balance and harmony in your life.

Now that you have made the overall commitment to yourself, it's time to make commitments to your goals. Perhaps you have done this in the past, but I encourage you to start fresh and do it again.

When setting goals, ensure they are specific and realistic. The more specific, the better! If you don't have a clear vision on what it is that you want, you may receive incorrect or unwanted versions of what you desire. You also want to be sure that what you desire aligns with your values and priorities.

I knew a woman who was trying everything in her power to find a soulmate. She dated guy after guy, but the relationships always seemed to end in disappointment. For months and months, I watched her get her heart broken over and over again. Each time, she felt more and more defeated, as though there was something wrong with her. Why was she attracting these incompatible men? She was doing the work physically, mentally, and emotionally. Yet she still found herself empty in this particular part of her life.

One night, when we were having a conversation, I asked her, "Where are you creating space for this person in your life? How clear are you on everything that you want in a soulmate?" I had noticed that she was asking for a man to come into her life, but that was it. There was no clear description of the exact man that she wanted. Not only that, but she did not have space physically in her life for this man.

We sat down together and wrote out a very clear description of her dream man. What were his attributes? Hair color, eye color, height, occupation, etc. We got down and dirty with every single detail. Next, she had to start creating space in her life. She cleaned out a portion of her closet. She left space in the bathroom cabinet. She turned down the side of the bed to indicate that she was looking for someone to sleep beside her. Within weeks, she met that man! He had every single characteristic that she had desired right down to the car he drove! They are now married and building dreams together. Sounds too good to be true, doesn't it?? Well, it's not. She is me!

There is power in physically writing out your goals. It sets an energetic motion into the world and also inserts them strongly into your own subconscious and focus. Without even being aware of it, you'll be focused on ways you can achieve them.

Once you have your goals written out, it'll be easier to create a plan for your vision. Ask yourself the following questions:

› Who do I need to get in front of?
› What books do I need to read?
› What mastermind groups do I need to join?
› What distractions do I need to get rid of?

Asking yourself these questions is part of the planning stage. Set a deadline for your answers as well. Deadlines aren't meant to hold you hostage but, rather, help with your own personal accountability.

My favorite thing to do each year is to update my vision board. There are many different ways to create a vision board, but all that matters is that you have one. If you're busy, I suggest using an application like Canva. It's quick, easy, and can be printed directly from the site and delivered right to your door. Put your vision board in a noticeable place so that, each day, you will see it and feel the excitement of reaching those desires and goals. You need to dream big here! No holding back. Nothing is off limits. Reach for the stars.

Be sure to share these goals with people that you know, love, and trust. This increases the energy being driven toward them. Not only will you be thinking about and envisioning your dreams coming true, but so will those who love and care about you. This also helps you stay on track and keeps you motivated to move forward. Remember, the aim of the vision board is to visualize success.

› What does it look like?
› What does it feel like?
› Who is around you when you achieve it?
› How has your life changed?

These visuals help you attach feelings to the thoughts, which creates the energetic momentum.

Another strategy for successfully achieving goals is the ninety-day personal inventory. Write out on a spreadsheet what action you need to take in the next ninety days to move closer to your goals. Then, every ninety days, review those goals from the previous ninety days and set new goals for the next ninety days. You can arrange your goals in the following six categories to have a birds-eye view of how each affects reaching the life of your dreams: mind, body, spirit, relationships, finances, and impact/experiences. I go into further detail about this exercise at serviceandsoul.com.

Answer the following questions to kick-start the momentum of your overall vision.

Mind: What do you want the future state of your mind to look like?

_____

_____

_____

_____

Body: Where does your physical self need to be in order to accomplish the long-term vision for your life?

_____

_____

_____

_____

_____

Spirit: What does the future state of your spiritual connection look like?

_____

_____

_____

_____

_____

Relationships: What do your future relationships look like?

_____

_____

_____

_____

_____

Finances: Where do your finances need to be to reach your long-term vision?

_____

Impact and Experiences: How do you want to change the world?

Roadblocks

My healing process hasn't always been giant strides forward. There have been setbacks, slips, and many roadblocks. Healing isn't linear; every single thing that happens to you, good or bad, is a chance to learn. Look for the opportunity in everything that comes your way. Look for the light. Teaching yourself to shift your perspective and look for what good can come out of every experience will cultivate growth in your life and organically allow things to change.

Slips, setbacks, and roadblocks are going to happen, and they are going to happen often. And that's okay! You are a human being living in a world with other human beings, and sometimes it gets messy.

Remember, you only have control over yourself. What matters is how you treat yourself during those moments. I talk to so many women who internally and externally berate themselves for not being perfect, for not facing every challenge perfectly, and for holding themselves to unreachable standards when going through the process. Let's be clear, no one is perfect or will ever be perfect. Believe that. Social media, unfortunately, gives you an unnatural perception of other people and their lives, and it's so easy to compare your story to someone else's. But they have their messy moments too. You may not see that on social media, but it's there. When you feel the urge to question your life and your worth, change direction and practice talking to yourself like you would a friend who was struggling.

Sometimes a slip can leave you feeling like you've made absolutely no progress. This is far from the truth! You don't lose all the momentum you have gained just because you made a mistake! *You are still on the path.* You are still on the journey to heal. Pick yourself up and keep going!

Where have you experienced a slip, setback, or roadblock lately? Write it down and announce it out loud for yourself. This will help you disempower the negative thoughts about the roadblock that threaten to paralyze you.

You're Worth It

Stop right here. Reread the subheading for this part. Are you wondering, "Am I worth it?" Yes. You are. Here's the thing about worthiness. You develop through childhood your own versions of what constitutes worthiness. Social media, peers, television, and movies have all shown you variations of worthiness. Even your family models what they deem worthy. It's no wonder you might walk around feeling like a fraud and a fake; you have constant internal conflict comparing yourself to what you have seen and what has been imprinted on you to form your beliefs around worthiness. I knew that when I wanted to start helping women heal, my work had to be centered around claiming worthiness because it's one of the most important topics for women's healing.

"Am I worthy?"

Worthiness comes from within. But with marketing, media, and other external forces undermining your innate worthiness, it's hard to tap into. So how do you become a being who walks around with your head held high? You cultivate your relationship with your inner self ... the intimate parts of your soul that form your internal guidance system ... the little voice inside that speaks to you.

Here's what took me a long time to really understand and apply to my own life. When you have a deep love for and connection to yourself, you navigate through difficult situations with ease. People are going to have perceptions and projections that they throw at you over which you have no control. If someone tells you that you are a fake or a fraud, and you believe it (even way deep down), you will hang on their comment and do an inventory on what you could've possibly done to make them feel that way. However, if you are deeply connected to yourself with love, you will show up and either acknowledge that maybe you have something you need to work on or that the other person is projecting something on you that they feel about themselves.

So what makes you feel worthy? Is it your job? Your relationship? Your motherhood?

It should be none of these! Beware of placing your worth in a particular role outside of yourself. Because the moment that you struggle in that area, you might determine that you have failed and sink into unworthiness. If the one thing that makes you feel worthy diminishes, your belief about your inherent worth can also diminish. But that's only a momentary belief—not the truth.

What's true is that you are a goddess. A woman who is right here, right now because you're longing for more. That in and of itself shows that you are worthy because you wouldn't fight for something that wasn't important to you! It's a waste of your resources. You are important to you! Be careful of the time and energy vampires that distract you from feeling worthy. It will happen, but now that you're prepared, you will be aware and you can fight it off with what is true!

On the following page are the stepping-stones of the decision, commitment, roadblocks, and belief in my own worth that I took along my individual journey. I find this visual of my experience still relevant when I have to make big life decisions or changes. Perhaps it will support you too.

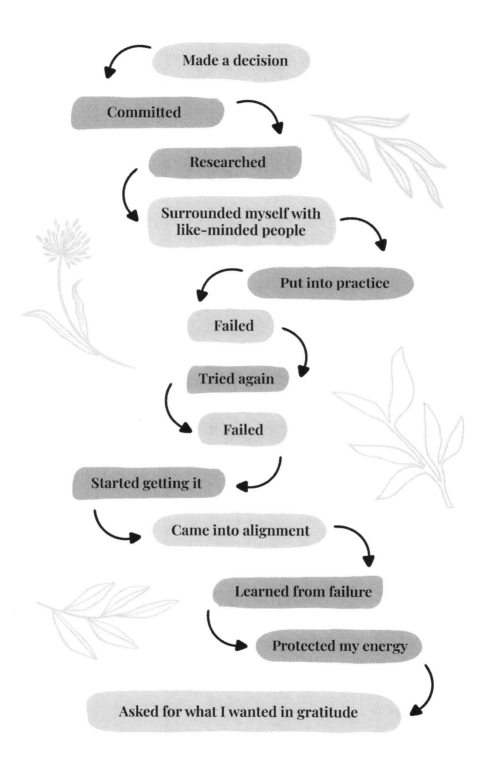

Made a decision

Committed

Researched

Surrounded myself with like-minded people

Put into practice

Failed

Tried again

Failed

Started getting it

Came into alignment

Learned from failure

Protected my energy

Asked for what I wanted in gratitude

CHAPTER 4
The "T" Word

In order to really get down to the root of what's holding you back, you have to start with the things that have created your beliefs. I once read the quote, "Heal the inner child, free yourself," and I remember not understanding what it meant. It just seemed like a *woo woo* way of making an excuse for certain behaviors that adults have.

I remember thinking, "How do I even talk to my inner child? What does she really have to say? What good will that do?" But, at the time, I had nothing to lose and nothing left but to try. When you are near or at rock-bottom, as you might be right now, you reach a point where you will try anything to feel something.

I was longing for understanding. I spent most of my life feeling like an impostor in my own skin. I was never taught how to properly process my thoughts and emotions. I don't blame my parents because they were never taught how to do it either. Thankfully, you now live in a time where you can break generational trauma and patterns that have been running in your family for ages. Breaking generational trauma means consciously and intentionally choosing to overcome negative patterns or behaviors that have been passed down within a family or community. Does this resonate with you?

Breaking generational trauma requires self-reflection, inner healing, and personal growth. It involves examining your beliefs, attitudes, and behaviors to identify any destructive patterns that you might have inherited. This self-awareness allows you to consciously choose a different path and make positive changes in your life. It's important to have a strong support system through a coach, counselor, or therapist for uncomfortable moments. It isn't easy turning your back on the norm that your family has had for many decades. It's a process that takes time and effort, but the rewards are profound as you pave the way for a healthier and more fulfilling future.

It's important to know that breaking generational trauma doesn't mean denying or disconnecting from your family history. Rather, you are consciously choosing to break the negative cycles. Draw strength from your roots, learn from the past, and use it as a catalyst for positive change. Remember, you have the ability to rewrite your story and create a positive legacy for yourself and your future generations.

Once I understood the power of breaking generational trauma, I felt a lot more freedom. It quickly became my mission because I didn't want my children to grow up without the understanding or belief in the power that they have to create the lives that they want.

I knew that it started with me.

When I learned about generational trauma and how it affects people as children, I was already a mother of a sixteen-year-old and an eleven-year-old. I remember thinking to myself, "I have screwed them up more than I realized." (I use that terminology lightly, of course.) It's not until you become a parent that you see your own parents as human beings who were also figuring it out as they went along. My parents were doing the best they could with what they knew and whatever resources they had. The difference for me is that I do know better now and can make the necessary changes as I see fit.

I became a mom at a very young age, so the notion that I likely had inflicted some childhood trauma onto my firstborn was not a surprise to me. In fact, it helped me release some of the pressure that I realized I was still holding onto as a mother. It allowed for a beautiful conversation with my son. I was able to sit with him and tell him what I had learned and give him permission to go through his own process of healing without feeling like he was betraying me in some way. In a sense, we grew up together. We had, and still have, a very close bond. I see him struggle with the fear of letting me down. It felt freeing for me, and hopefully for him too, to give him permission to confront me for his own healing without having to necessarily drag me down or talk badly about me to a stranger in a therapist's office one day.

When you experience trauma as a child, you stay at that age emotionally until you heal it. Though you continue to grow physically and intellectually, your nervous system reacts like your broken younger self who feels wounded, hurt, and out of control. Because trauma influences your ability to regulate emotions effectively, you might walk around with the emotional intellect of a wounded child. You may struggle with intense emotions and experience frequent mood swings, anger, sadness, or anxiety. Your emotional responses may be heightened or unpredictable, making it challenging to navigate relationships and daily life.

Many couples in the military world married young. And you unknowingly brought your childhood trauma into your precious young marriages. You didn't allow yourself the time to learn who you really were so that you could be a better version of yourself for someone that you loved. All of the negative beliefs that I had built up about my unworthiness, inadequacy, and being undeserving of love and support came barrel rolling into my marriage, causing conflict almost immediately. But the trauma that I brought into my marriage also made it easier for me to dissolve into my then-husband as quickly as possible. My life started revolving around him and his career and me being the perfect stay-at-home wife and mother. I thought I was healing, but I was actually losing myself. I lost my purpose, I lost my identity, and I lost my confidence *as an individual*. I was also foisting my insecurities onto him and my children.

Trauma can impact your ability to trust and feel safe in relationships. Left unhealed, these wounds can hinder your ability to create healthy connections with others. You may fail to form secure attachments and struggle with intimacy and vulnerability, which can further impede your emotional growth.

Overcoming the impediments caused by trauma is imperative to strengthen connections and mature emotionally. But it is a challenge. There is no right or wrong way to heal. You have your own path, and it is not linear. You might heal through a lot of self-reflection using coaching, books, and healing retreats. Or you may need more support through a counselor or therapist. Don't be afraid to try out many resources and keep trying until you find the best fit. I have many that helped me at serviceandsoul.com.

To jumpstart your healing, first identify sources and times of your trauma. In what ways do you see trauma show up in your life? Reflect on your childhood as if watching a film of it. Can you pinpoint traumatic situations? Can you see your inner child lashing out from fear, pain, and grief? This is a painful exercise. But stick with it because understanding and addressing your trauma is critical to feeling truly free within yourself. A beautiful aspect of this process is that not only are you releasing emotional trauma and pain, but you are also becoming more one with your physical body.

Trauma has a tremendous physical effect on your body. You might hold it through tension and chronic pain. Or it may manifest as a lack of rest and overall sleep, digestive problems, autoimmune disease, and even cardiovascular issues. I first learned about this connection from a book called *The Body Keeps the Score: Brain,*

Mind, and Body in the Healing of Trauma, by psychiatrist Bessel van der Kolk. In this book, Dr. van der Kolk talks about the scientific and philosophical approaches to the connection of the mind and body. He explains how traumatic stress is associated with functional and chemical changes in the emotional part of the brain. Thanks to this book and the consequent uptick in the research behind the mind-body connection, you now have an extraordinary opportunity to understand how to connect intimately with your body and heal your trauma to feel better. Do you have physical experiences that may be linked to trauma? (Please note that I am not a medical professional; consult with healthcare professionals who can provide proper assessment, guidance, and treatment options.)

There are four major forms of childhood trauma—rejection, betrayal, abandonment, and injustice. Let's discuss each so that you can acknowledge them and start to move through them.

Rejection

It's likely that you struggle from rejection if you constantly draw assumptions about what other people think about you. I relate most to this. I've been told throughout my lifetime that I take things way too personally and that I make assumptions about how other people think and feel about me. And you know what, it is one hundred percent true! I'm blessed to now be fully aware of it, and I am able to work each day on healing the rejection that the little girl inside of me feels.

Typically, if you struggle with rejection trauma, you are very wary of letting people in. Why? Because it feels unsafe. If you let people in, they will come to know the real you, and then they may reject you. It's an internal war; you constantly wonder what other people think about you, so it's easier not to let them in.

If you are a fellow people pleaser, it is also likely that rejection was your trauma. You tend to suffer in silence because you fear that if you express your feelings, you will be rejected as needing everything to be about you. You make it your life's work to be a people pleaser for a very self-serving reason. If you can make everyone else's life better, then people will like you, and you won't have to deal with rejection. Because people pleasers never deal with rejection, right?! Wrong! Even as I write this book, I am going through a rejection from a very close friend whose own childhood trauma conflicted with mine and caused toxicity between us.

Here are some powerful affirmations for healing rejection. Read them, write them, say them, feel them.

› Positive energy nourishes my body and helps me radiate joy to others.
› A happy, joyful life is being created for me right now.
› I attract an abundance of every good thing God has for me: relationships, opportunities, financial stability, career success, love, and great health.
› I do not allow past hurt or disappointments to prevent me from trying again.
› I do not chase any person or any opportunity. My opportunities and connections are authentic, and I attract them in an organic way.
› I trust the process and embrace the journey. Regardless of what I see in this present moment, I know that the best is yet to come. I celebrate each and every breakthrough right now. I look forward with eagerness for the things to come and to reflecting back on this time with a heart full of gratitude.

Which affirmation speaks the most to you? Write it out and put it somewhere where you can see it every day. Speak it and feel it into your new experiences!

Betrayal

Betrayal is a nasty trauma. If you relate to betrayal trauma, you might have trouble recognizing, expressing, or managing your emotions. You might feel like you're all over the place! Your mind will constantly change because you cannot trust the environment that you're in. Anxiety, depression, and other mental health symptoms can arise from this type of trauma. If you experienced betrayal, you could find yourself struggling in relationships, feeling emotionally numb, and suffering nightmares and anxiety on a regular basis.

Betrayal is painful! As you read this, do you feel emotion rising up in your body? Everyone has experienced betrayal in some way. And let's be honest … Everyone, unfortunately, has betrayed others. But those who have a deep-rooted betrayal trauma can struggle with trust. Lacking trust can manifest in different ways and impact your relationships with others and yourself. You might be suspicious, have difficulty relying on others, be extra guarded or emotionally distant, fear intimacy, have a constant need for control, or have difficulty forgiving and moving on.

You can rebuild trust, but it takes time and effort, both with yourself and with others. You must gradually forge understandings, set boundaries, and be open and honest when you communicate.

Here are some affirmations for healing betrayal. Read them, write them, say them, feel them.

> › Every challenge I face is an opportunity to grow and improve.
> › My contributions are unique and meaningful.
> › Today, I forgive myself for any and all past mistakes. And I forgive others for their mistakes. When I forgive others, I get better at forgiving myself.

Abandonment

Abandonment trauma is one of the more prevalent types of trauma. If you struggle with abandonment trauma from childhood, you'll have an ongoing fear of experiencing abandonment again. As an adult, you may struggle to form healthy relationships, leading to low self-esteem, low self-worth, and depression. When you have abandonment trauma, you feel like it's hard to trust others or build lasting connections. You may even abandon yourself, which can manifest as loneliness, emptiness, or a longing for nurturing and care.

I didn't experience abandonment trauma until I was a military spouse. Having a spouse who was constantly deploying or gone for weeks upon weeks of training triggered my feelings of abandonment. It felt like a huge void in the house, leaving me feeling unsupported and alone. I also felt emotionally disconnected since we weren't able to communicate as much or as often as we wanted to.

As a military spouse, I felt like I didn't have a true support system, which amplified my abandonment trauma. My friends who were also military spouses were going through their own struggles, so I felt like leaning on them would just be further piling on. And anyone outside of the military world would never be able to fully understand or grasp the amount of loneliness that comes from having a spouse in the service.

Here are some great affirmations to help move through your abandonment trauma. Read them, write them, say them, feel them.

> › All my words, thoughts, and actions are divinely guided and protected.
> › God will guide me on anything and everything divinely.
> › I am capable of creating healthy, lasting relationships.

› I am lovable and deserving of love.
› I am ready to let go of my fear of abandonment.

Injustice

Injustice trauma can be caused by various experiences and situations that involve unfair treatment, discrimination, family dysfunction, societal trauma, bullying, harassment, or violations of basic human rights including abuse, violence, and oppression. I was surprised to learn from my research that this form of trauma can occur indirectly to a child and affect them as an adult. According to the National Center for PTSD, a child may see a parent affected by injustice and begin to act the same way as the parent in order to feel connected. Similarly, when a child feels that they need to step up and act as a parent due to their parent suffering trauma symptoms, the child may, over time, end up having those same symptoms.

If you suffered injustice as a child, it is likely that you feel physical pain in your body. You might feel fatigued or drained on a regular basis. Your emotions could be very unpredictable and overall irrational. You might even struggle with short-term attention span conditions like ADD or ADHD.

Affirmations for injustice follow. Read them, write them, say them, feel them.

› I deserve to feel safe, comfortable, and confident in this body.
› I accept myself the way I am; my body is perfect the way it is.
› I deserve to be loved and respected.
› I trust myself and my instincts.
› I trust myself to make the right decisions for me.

All of the characteristics that you possess based on your past traumas are defense mechanisms that have been created subconsciously. How do they show up in your life? When you fail to acknowledge and validate these traumas, you (even as an adult) fear rejection, betrayal, abandonment, or some sort of injustice in every relationship. This mindset will become a self-fulfilling prophecy. Remember, everything that you focus on expands. If you constantly walk around in your childhood trauma, then you bring focus to that exact feeling and you will attract the same experience. Have you noticed that a lot of your relationships end in the same pattern? The only way to change course is to acknowledge the inner child, understand what she wants to say, and love her through her own healing experience.

Nurturing and healing the wounded parts of yourself that may have experienced neglect, trauma, or unmet needs in the past is a powerful process! Cultivate self-compassion and an understanding attitude and treat yourself just as kind as you would another child. Acknowledge that the pain and the trauma that you experienced were not your fault and that you do deserve love, validation, and healing.

Take time to connect with your inner child through visualization or meditation. Imagine your younger self, and talk to her. Establish that loving connection, and then sit in quiet and listen to what she needs. Create a safe space for her to express her feelings and experiences. Allow yourself to fully feel and express them even if it seems a little overwhelming. Use this as an opportunity to validate the emotions of your inner child, and reassure her that she is seen, heard, and loved. This is a powerful way to identify the needs that were not met during your childhood and devise healthier ways to nurture them, like self-care, establishing healthy boundaries, and creating a supportive community of friends that meets your emotional, physical, and spiritual needs.

I remember the first time that I ever did an inner child healing. I got in a quiet space, sat down, and closed my eyes. I took a moment to really get my mind in a place to have a beautiful healing experience. I took a few deep breaths and asked her to come into that space with me. I immediately saw sweet, adorable, and innocent six-year-old little Jenna. It was such a powerful moment that I truly will never forget. I remember the look on her face of longing for support, love, and comfort. It was through this experience that I learned how deep the feeling of belonging is for me. I realized that all I've ever wanted was to feel like I belonged. I was able to recognize all of the times where I acted out and got loud just to gain attention or to try and fit in. With this new awareness, I now know how to belong within myself. What a beautiful gift! It has taken me a lot of years, but it has been worth everything that I have poured into myself to get to where I am today. I now am able to acknowledge when my inner child starts to feel like she doesn't belong. I am able to communicate to her all of the things that make her fully belong.

The same confidence and peace that I have built internally is also attainable for you, my sweet friend.

CHAPTER 5
Feminine Power

Let's talk about feminine power—that thing that neither society, your momma, nor your religious leaders talked about. You often don't cultivate your feminine power consciously. You learn how to be a wife by what you've seen. You learn how to be a mother by what you've seen. You learn your definitions of what's beautiful by what you've seen. Your beliefs about feminine power are modeled to you from a young age and you don't even know it's happening. It's the programming that you received by watching the other women in your life as you grew up.

This chapter is designed to help you erase the programming that you have unconsciously picked up so that you can consciously step into your feminine power. Here, you'll identify the different parts of you, and you'll learn to choose which parts to harness. This understanding will allow you to become conscious and intentionally make choices rather than absorbing the programming around you.

Feminine power is a collection of different internal qualities that allow you the opportunity to bring balance (or create chaos) in your life. You know, those voices in your head that argue back and forth while you are trying to get some sleep! It's the voice in your head telling you to stick it to the man or that you should become invisible because you feel threatened. You have different layers of femininity that fight for space in your consciousness.

I wasn't raised with a ton of feminine power in the traditional sense. My mom was an only child raised on a working farm. She wasn't ever taught to rise into her feminine power, so I can't blame her for not knowing how to teach that to me. It wasn't until later in my life that I really learned the different levels of femininity. Many coaches and healers have different titles for these different parts. You may have heard terms like divine feminine, dark feminine, seductress, lover, wife, mother, teacher, sister, etc. I proudly wear a lot of these feminine labels. I am a mom, I am a wife, I am a sister, I am a seductress to my husband, I am a lover.

The ones that I refer to in this book are the Little Girl, the Princess, the Queen, and the Divine Queen. Before I introduce you to these four different levels, I want to be very clear that these are not identities that I have created myself. They have been created over many generations of the female collective. Through much inner discovery and acknowledgment of the collective, they have been categorized into these four different spaces so that you can tend to them individually.

I'll go into depth about the differences between the four levels of femininity, but I must warn you that once you learn about them, once you have the knowledge of what I'm about to share with you, your entire outlook on situations and experiences is going to change. You will have no other choice but to call your Divine Queen to rise in every situation. Coming to understand these four levels of femininity in my own life has had an irrevocable impact on my personal interactions, conversations, and, most importantly, relationships I have with myself and other women.

So are you ready?

The Little Girl

The Little Girl—the sweet precious Little Girl. She's needy and wants to be taken care of. She's entitled and thinks the world is to blame for her problems. She walks around with a victim mentality because it serves her so well. She complains a lot. She doesn't learn, evolve, or grow because she doesn't need to. If she's a "good girl," she'll get what she wants. She relies on coping mechanisms, such as drugs and alcohol or sex. She's constantly trying to escape because she doesn't really know herself. She's very insecure. Her physical body leads the way. Everything in her world is superficial, and she cannot control her emotions.

Recently, I was in an airport in Fort Lauderdale. My connecting flight back home had been delayed two hours. Although out of everyone's control, many people were rattled by the unknown: how long we would have to wait. The missing crew member finally arrived, and everyone cheered out of relief. I went to the bathroom and, while I was in there, I heard a little girl around eighteen months old screaming at the top of her lungs out of pure frustration. I chuckled, and I thought about how many of us waiting for our flight resembled this little girl in her moment of frustration.

How many times do you, as an adult, wish that you could scream and pout and have someone soothe you and say, "Awe, poor girl, she's probably had a rough day?" There are moments in your life where your Little Girl shows up wanting empathy, but, since you are a grown-up, you can't throw a tantrum and expect other people to make you feel better. You need to learn to verbalize her frustrations and soothe her yourself.

Where do you see the Little Girl show up in your life? When I feel like I'm being talked over or not acknowledged, I typically see my Little Girl because she wants attention and reassurance. Now that I'm able to recognize her, I can nurture her through my Divine Queen so that she feels seen and acknowledged and doesn't have to act out in response to her fears. This is not easy to do, and you need to be gentle and patient with yourself while you practice coming to know her and what she needs.

Last year, I attended a retreat where I worked with my inner Little Girl. I learned how to connect to her so that she felt seen and heard. I also learned how to recognize the positive ways in which she shows up. For example, I spent a morning in the ocean alone in presence. While I floated in the water, I checked in with my Little Girl and asked, "What do you want to do right now?" Without skipping a beat, she said, "Oh I want to do flips! And I want to swim like a mermaid! And I want to do cannonballs into the water!!!" So guess what? I did just that and had *so much fun*!! I realized in that moment that if I check on and nurture this part of me, the Little Girl will show me ways to have fun and joy.

The Princess

Learning about the Princess was quite comical because, at least in my generation, being a "princess" was something girls sought and would hopefully one day become. A princess was the pinnacle of life and femininity. Disney fairytale b.s. taught me that I needed to wait for my prince to ride in on a white horse, save me, and give me things without really having to work for them. Being a princess meant that I would be taken care of and that I would not have to take care of anyone else. The Princess *deserves* to be taken care of after paying her dues.

The Princess is very overprotective, demanding, controlling, and competitive. She often lacks girlfriends because she doesn't trust them (nor do they trust her). She constantly compares herself to others, both those who are more successful than she is and those who are less successful. A know-it-all, she's hard on others and makes them feel inadequate so that she can feel like she is valuable because she's "better" than them.

This next realization hit me hard. With the Princess, partners and children only feel *conditional* love.

Wow.

When I learned about the Princess, my first reaction was denial. Remember the story I told you about wanting to fight with my then-husband and make him pay for what he had done to me without any self-reflection? Princess. I finally accepted that I've spent most of my adult life in the Princess mentality. When I heard it explained and it resonated, I desperately tried to find some sort of "out," to not have to acknowledge my truth and take responsibility for it.

I have, however, come to accept and appreciate the Princess; she has shown up for me in the past couple of years while I've transitioned through some life stages. See, while many of her attributes are negative, the Princess is really here to protect you. She's the one that stands up and says, "You're not gonna treat me that way!" Or, "I don't need you! I'm a boss babe who can do it on my own!" But the problem is that the tone usually masks a negative self-reflection. It leads to blame-shifting that creates conflict between the Princess and herself as well as between the Princess and the target of her deep anger.

When the Princess appears in my life now, I thank her lovingly for wanting to keep me safe, but ask her to allow the Queen to rise up and claim the fairness that she seeks. Whenever I make room for my Queen, I always feel powerful rather than powerless. The Princess likes to stir up drama. She likes to ruffle feathers. She likes to point out others' faults so that she doesn't have to acknowledge her own. But when you allow the Queen to take control in a loving way, not only will you experience greater self-control and personal growth, you will also emerge from a situation with your head held high and with improved self-esteem. Asking the Princess to step down from her pedestal and out of the spotlight allows you to lean into the higher vibration of the life of your dreams.

In what ways do you see your Princess show up?

The Queen

The Queen arises when you have an awakening and connect with your inner femininity. It's when you feel deep down in your soul, "I have arrived!" The Queen knows that everything that happens is happening *for* her, not *to* her. She is wise, both in mind and heart. She has *emotional intelligence*. Her top priority is to bring love into herself. She leads with honesty and integrity. She's patient. She's accepting. She is radiant and beautiful. She shows unconditional love. She's kind, compassionate, and captivating! She embraces other women and encourages them to rise in their own individual power. She knows her purpose, and she makes a difference in the world.

When I first discovered the attributes of the Queen, I knew that I wanted her to lead from then on. Once I had this knowledge, there were no more excuses for not bringing myself into a higher awareness, vibration, and knowing. I could no longer allow my Princess to ruin relationships or opportunities. I knew that I had a Queen inside me who could not only accomplish the very things the Princess desired, but could do so in a way that would have positive lasting effects on all who encountered her.

The Divine Queen

As if the Queen isn't glorious enough, there's one more step—the Divine Queen.

The Divine Queen is the ultimate highest self. She honors all life. She recognizes she is in this world but not *of* this world. She is both earthly and heavenly. She's magnetic. She attracts everything with her essence. She shines unapologetically, and she has a well-run Queendom. She is cosmically attractive. She possesses a silent power, not loud and obtrusive. She lives for her purpose and embraces her "too muchness."

The Divine Queen makes no excuses and no justifications because she doesn't need to.

Imagine your life as a Divine Queen!

I hope you're as excited after reading about the four levels of femininity as I was when I first learned about them. I hope you begin to recognize and hunger for your Divine Queen. As I said before, this is not going to be easy. But the Divine Queen consistently works on her growth. Just because she embodies the highest level of femininity and self doesn't mean that she is "done."

So where are you learning? How are you growing into your Divine Queen?

When you look at life as a constant opportunity for learning and growth, you will become more aligned and in tune with your inner spirit and divine essence.

Yes, it can be scary. Yes, you will make mistakes.

But you can become everything you ever dreamed of becoming. The power is yours.

At the beginning of this journey, the Little Girl and the Princess may be the roles you feel safest in, but, as you implement the tools that I'm going to share through the rest of this book, you're going to see the Queen and the Divine Queen rise!

CHAPTER 6
Warrior > Worrier

Early on in their healing journeys, many Princesses cannot relinquish control to their Queens. I help the women I work with navigate this by teaching them to understand that the Princess is not wrong. She needs to be acknowledged and have her fears validated so that she doesn't feel unseen. She's scared and uncertain, and that's okay. This is where you start shifting from the worrier to the warrior. After I made the decision and commitment that I wanted to make a change in my life, I nurtured my Princess to become a warrior.

Where do you find yourself at this current moment? Are you constantly consumed by fear and anxiety, always worried about the future and what might happen? Do you feel powerless and overwhelmed by your circumstances? Are you struggling to find joy and meaning? Are you a worrier?

When you approach life as a worrier, you find yourself stuck. Stuck in a cycle of fear and negativity, unable to move forward to create the life you truly desire. But when you embrace your inner warrior, you awaken the strength and courage that can help you overcome anything that gets in your way.

Being a warrior does not mean that you'll never have setbacks, fears, or uncertainty. It just means that you have a choice during moments of resistance. You can choose to face your fears with courage and determination. You can trust your own abilities and trust in your higher power to guide you.

There are a great deal of resources available as you start your healing journey. You may have already done some searching and found resources like meditation, therapy, counseling (yes, there's a difference), books, podcasts, etc. But what's right for someone else may not be right for you. Afterall, your journey is yours and yours alone. That's why I created courses and retreats to help women like you dive in to find what works best for you! Be sure to go to serviceandsoul.com for the free resources I have for you there.

I remember when I first started trying to meditate. I would frustratingly think, "What a joke! You mean to tell me that people do this on a regular basis and are able to clear their minds and look out of their third eye?" I laugh about my reaction now because meditation became an important part of my growth. But when I first started, I had resisted because I was applying other people's rules for how I was supposed to do it. Meditation can be done in so many different ways. Whether you're sitting crossed-legged on the floor with your eyes closed in complete om or lying in your bed visualizing the life that you want, you are meditating. I personally love visualization meditations. They resonate most with me and my soul. In time, you will learn what works best for you!

There are other great modalities that I also recommend, such as breathwork, Kundalini, and Reiki. There is something for everyone at every budget.

Meditation

Meditation is a beautiful practice that brings about a sense of calm and peace. While you may, at first, struggle with being still, you can eliminate some of that pressure. You don't have to sit in complete stillness and silence. You can instead focus your attention on a particular object in the room, a vision of your future desire, or even an activity you enjoy doing to connect with the present moment. The goal is to quiet the many thoughts you have regularly running through your mind. The word meditation literally means "to become familiar with." Think of it as allowing yourself to look within at all of the thoughts, behaviors, and emotions that you have inside. It's an opportunity to retire the old limiting negative beliefs and create new positive ones that resonate with you and your goals and dreams.

Overall, meditation helps reduce stress and promote relaxation, which has a positive impact on mental and physical health. It improves focus and concentration, boosts the immune system, and enhances overall well-being.

Breathwork

Breathwork and meditation often go hand-in-hand. Breathwork helps you connect more deeply with your body and the way that you *feel*. It intentionally forces you to manipulate your breath in different ways to bring about specific physical, mental, and emotional effects. The reason this modality is so successful and powerful is because it directly affects the vagus nerve, which is the largest nerve in the parasympathetic nervous system. The vagus nerve plays a vital role in regulating your stress response and helping you to feel calm and relaxed. Participating in breath work and other relaxation techniques helps to stimulate the vagus nerve to calm you inside and outside.

Breathwork typically focuses on slow, deep breathing or specific breathing patterns that help you shift your energy. As you do these different types of breathing techniques, you'll notice physical sensations in your body almost immediately. I noticed that my hands would clench into a fist as a sort of prelude to a beautiful emotional release. Everybody experiences breathwork differently, but it is a valuable practice in learning how to ground oneself.

Kundalini

Kundalini is a step up from breathwork because it also involves bodily movement. The purpose of Kundalini is to activate the energy at the base of your spine. In this practice, you move through different types of postures and breathing exercises to help release tension in your body and improve circulation. You'll likely feel a sense of empowerment and vitality as you practice Kundalini. Just like meditation and breathwork, Kundalini helps relieve stress and improve focus, but it can also help you connect with your higher self and tap into a deeper sense of inner peace and wisdom. Kundalini wakes up a dormant energy that you have inside your body. While practicing it, you will likely experience a deep sense of peace and connection to something greater than yourself. This can help you cultivate compassion, gratitude, and humility and allow you to tap into the divine wisdom and guidance that is always available to you. Kundalini allows you to overcome old patterns of thought and behavior and create new positive ones.

Reiki

Practicing Reiki is all about energy. Reiki is done with a certified Reiki practitioner who is trained to help channel energy to specific areas of your body. The first few times that I tried Reiki, I couldn't believe that something as simple as gentle touch or non-contact techniques would have any impact on me, but I was wrong!

Reiki sessions are beautiful and deeply relaxing. They help you release tension, balance your energy, and promote healing on physical, emotional, and spiritual levels. Typically, during a session, you lie on a massage table fully clothed. The practitioner places their hands on or just above different parts of your body near your chakras. This process sets an intention for the session and invokes the healing energy of the Reiki.

The practitioner may find themselves energetically drawn to a specific area where they feel like you may be blocked or stagnant. As energy from their hands flows into your body, you may feel sensations of warmth, tingling, or relaxation. I've even been known to fall asleep!

If you feel like Reiki might be out of your comfort zone, just know that any seasoned practitioner will ask you what your preferences are and move through the sessions at your own comfort level, so don't be afraid to give it a try.

Along with reducing stress and amplifying overall calmness, Reiki is a tool for spiritual growth and transformation. It helps you connect with your inner self and tap into the deeper purpose and meaning of your life. Practicing Reiki helped me truly be able to see, feel, and connect with God in such a deep way. I once had an amazing session where I felt this overwhelming feeling of true unconditional love. It was so powerful that I wept in pure love and joy! When we finished that session, the practitioner said to me, "That is God within you, and you can access Him anytime, anywhere!" It is something that I practice regularly to keep me in alignment with myself and with God. Reiki allows me to show myself greater compassion, which then enables me to bring that to the outside world.

As you lean into these different types of healing modalities, you will start attracting more like-minded people who are on a similar journey. Because, remember, like attracts like.

Like Attracts Like

Have you ever heard the phrase, "Show me the people you spend the most time with and I will show you your future?" The people that you spend your time around are the people that you're going to be the most like. The best advice that I ever received was to spend time with people who lived the same life that I wanted to create for myself. Early in my healing journey, I dismissed my own worth, thinking things like, "I don't have anything to offer them" or "Why would they want to spend their time with me?" But there is nothing more attractive to a successful person than another person who is hungry to learn and grow from them. Healed people like healing people, and successful people like helping people become successful.

Think about the people that you spend the most time with. Is there someone in your life who might be deadweight? Someone holding you back from moving forward? Someone who doesn't encourage or motivate you to make growth decisions? Someone who doesn't treat others the way you do. "But I've been friends with them for such a long time!" That was always my excuse for holding onto them. But if the relationship no longer serves you, it's time to move on. And you can do so with all the love and light in the world. You may be thinking, "But I don't want to be alone." While you might be alone for a little while, you won't be for long. Before you know it, you will attract other like-minded people who want the same growth that you seek.

Spend time with people who are present, attuned, and hungry for growth. Notice I didn't say perfect. You are not looking for perfection, only people who have what you want and live the life you want to live. Spending time with these people will help you put into practice all of the things that you're learning and researching to help you move to the next level in your life.

Accountability

Allow these important people in your life to hold you accountable. Accountability underlies your deepest and most valuable friendships. Gone are the days of having friends who only tell you what you want to hear. There is no growth in that! All that leaves you is stuck. Perhaps you have a current friend who placates you. They are not a bad person, nor do you have to ditch them because now you're too good for them. If you have friends that you love and cherish, and they love and cherish you, have a conversation with them. Ask them to hold you accountable, and give them permission to be honest with you. Let them in on this new change that you want to make. Who knows, you might even inspire them to go on their own growth journey. There's power in sharing your dreams, hopes, and desires with your nearest and dearest. Chances are, there's at least one friend that feels the same pull as you and will be relieved to know that you can walk this journey together.

I understand that it can be scary at first to allow other people into your life to hold you accountable. But I encourage you because of how truly powerful authentic accountability partnerships can be. They allow you to be clear about your intentions and define specific actions that might be holding you back. It can be hard to be real with yourself. You have blindspots and blinkers, and sometimes it's easier to look the other way in the short run. But, in the long run, those easy outs will halt your momentum. That's why it's so important to have select people that you know and trust to call you out and to encourage you to push through the roadblocks and setbacks that you are bound to experience. I found such accountability-oriented friends in mastermind groups.

Mastermind Groups

Joining mastermind groups created considerable shifts in my life as I was instantly surrounded by like-minded people moving in my same direction and no longer surrounded by people who weren't in alignment with the desires of my heart. Masterminds don't have to be an already-established group, cost lots of money, or require you to specialize in anything specific. You can start your own mastermind group by reaching out to people within your sphere of influence. Maybe there is someone that you've been wanting to work with or learn from for a while. Creating a mastermind is the perfect opportunity to reach out to them.

I have been a part of several life-changing mastermind groups. My very first group cost $14,000 for the year. I was a brand-new business owner and did not have $14,000. Yet I moved through that fear and signed the contract without looking back. I remember calling my husband in tears because I was so afraid. I was afraid that I wouldn't find the money. I was afraid that I wasn't worth it. I mean, who was I to think that I was worth investing in financially? When you live more than a decade making sure that you spend your time, money, and energy on your family to keep things calm and organized as your sacrifice to the military, you rarely spend money on yourself.

Moreover, I was afraid that it wasn't going to help. But I was wrong. Not only did I grow an incredible business during that time, I also showed myself that I was worth investing in. Since then, I have consistently invested in different mastermind groups that are centered around my goals.

I'm currently part of a mastermind group called G-FORCE that was established to bring entrepreneurs together to create businesses that are a force for good (hence the name). In just the last several months, I have not only been able to build an incredible community to hold me accountable, I've also learned effective systems and processes to help me grow professionally and personally. Each week, we gather to share ideas and collaborate on projects. We also assist one another with advice and solutions when navigating through obstacles. I am now surrounded with people whose sole purpose is not to get rich, but to make a difference in the lives and businesses of others.

Being part of a group like this offers support and accountability because I'm able to participate with others who operate with the same mindset. Having a safe place to share my goals, challenges, and progress is helpful in keeping my momentum.

Mastermind groups are also excellent spaces for networking. They lead to new opportunities, partnerships, and even collaborations.

One of my mastermind colleagues decided that she wanted to have a networking group for women entrepreneurs centered around organic and authentic business connections. So she started a group, which now hosts two events every month in thirteen different cities for women who are hungry for growth, connection, and collaboration. I'm blessed to have been a part of this growth and love watching it continue to reach and bless others.

Through this group, I get to help women in my community network with other local women who are stepping into their purpose and following their dreams. Each and every time that we gather, I watch the magic happen. One of our networking partners had a dream of opening up a women's co-working space. Though she didn't know how to launch it or grow it, she knew that she had the right women around her to help her accomplish it. Now she has a thriving and safe space in which women can work and create. Could she have done it without being part of our women's networking group? Definitely! Do you think she is grateful that she didn't have to figure it out on her own? You bet! Surrounding yourself with people who share your dreams and ambition is one of the greatest gifts that you can give yourself. If you're looking for a group of like-minded women who are military and first responder wives, be sure to join the Facebook Service and Soul group.

Acting "As If"

Acting "as if" is showing up today with the mindset that you're already where you want to be. Don't get it confused with "fake it 'til you make it." There's nothing fake about this, sister. You are walking the walk and showing up as if you are already the top producer in your industry, the most successful cookie-maker in town, or the go-to gal for people's financial planning. Whatever it is that your desire calls for, you show up as that person every single day. You *feel* her. You *become* her. You *are* her! Do not focus on the ways in which you currently lack that position. All that does is create drama and chaos around the things that you really want.

One of the simplest exercises that I have my clients do is called the warrior pose. Think of it as a strong goddess who commands the attention of the room without even trying. She stands tall, she's strong, she exudes confidence, she doesn't waste her energy on things that don't serve her, she knows who she is! You don't need to have all of the things to be her. You can be her right now, today!

The power of showing up "as if" creates an energetic belief that tells the universe that you are ready to move into the next level of life. It's an unshakable belief that you trust in your abilities and have the utmost confidence in all of your decisions.

> When you show up "as if," you prove that you believe in yourself.
> You take responsibility for your actions.
> You embrace the challenges, and you learn from them.
> You face your fears head on and challenge yourself to push beyond your limits.
> You're resilient.
> You bounce back from setbacks, and you never give up.
> You keep moving forward even when it gets tough.
> You practice self-discipline and follow through with your commitment and goals even when it's difficult.
> You stand up for what you believe in and fight for your principles.
> You speak the truth even if it's unpopular.
> You're compassionate to yourself and others.
> You understand that everyone has their struggles, and you approach them with empathy and kindness.

Remember, being a warrior is a mindset. It's about showing up every day with courage and determination even in the face of adversity!

CHAPTER 7
Self*ISH*

I was raised in the South, where you said "Yes ma'am" and "Yes sir," and you didn't do anything without asking yourself how it might affect someone else. You were taught at a very young age to put others first. My good ol' southern mamma frequently said, "Now don't be selfish!" It's astonishing to look back at how many times I heard that as a child. Even as a mother, I remember many times where I would try to teach my own children a lesson on how to share by admonishing them to not be "selfish." There was always a negative connotation with that word. If you ever made anything about yourself, you were self-centered and didn't care about other people. There's a good chance that if you struggle with self-care, it's because you fear being considered "selfish." For a very long time, "selfish" was a huge trigger word for me. What I want to help normalize in this chapter is the difference between being selfish and being self*ISH*.

Selfishness is defined as putting your own interests or happiness above that of others. As a child, I learned that anyone who did something for themselves was surely making someone else feel worse for their own gain. Selfishness was always linked to someone else's feelings or emotions. And I was taught to put other people's feelings above my own, no matter the cost to me. It's no wonder that I coped by being a people pleaser. My fears of being selfish were further amplified when I married a military man. When your spouse is selflessly serving your country, any perceived act of selfishness is to be strictly avoided. Many spouses of service members feel whiplash because they're told that caretakers need to make time for self-care, while simultaneously being shamed for doing anything for themselves.

I've finally learned that the difference between selfishness and being self*ISH* is intention. To be self*ISH* means that you are setting an intention for the purpose of growth, healing, and freedom. It's about you and your needs. It's taking an inventory of your life and taking action toward making yourself a better person and learning how to better connect yourself to the world that you desire to be part of. It's why airlines tell you to put the oxygen mask on yourself first. If you don't do that, you are of no use to anyone else.

Though it might be tough for some of you to swallow, it is a very important step in the process of healing. Once you're able to acknowledge the difference between selfishness and being self*ISH*, you will find that you show up more for people in an authentic way than you ever have before. It's not about taking from others; it's about giving to yourself.

Presence

I was raised by a hard-working, successful mother who was raised by a hard-working, successful father. I carried the things that I saw in my childhood into my adult life. I thought that in order to look successful to others, I had to have a full schedule. I believed that the only way that I would get empathy or attention was to completely overwork myself and constantly be *doing*. But I'm not a human *doing*. I'm a human *being*.

Last year, I decided to take a leap into the unknown and attend a silent retreat that was very appropriately called "Presence." It was a weeklong retreat where we abandoned our phones, computers, books, and, yes, even our voices, so we could learn the power of being present. This was not easy for me, someone who loves to talk and connect with people. There were around nineteen of us there, some people I knew, some I didn't. It felt strange to be around women I didn't know and not be able to talk to them to get to know them. But something remarkable happened. I felt like I knew them better at the end of the week by not talking to them! We put all of the gab and masks aside and looked each other in the eyes and *saw* one another. Have you ever stared into someone else's eyes without speaking? It is a soul experience, a moment of genuine connection because you look past the veils and disguises and into another person's shadows and truth to see who they really are.

Throughout that week, we learned how to sit with our thoughts and feelings even if they were uncomfortable. By becoming present, we were able to see things we normally wouldn't see. We were able to hear things we normally wouldn't hear. We were mindful and actually experienced our food while eating it. At the end of the week, when we got our devices back, I didn't turn mine on for hours because I wasn't ready to give up that feeling of being grounded, connected, and present. Through that retreat, I learned how to set boundaries around things that deserve my time and attention so that I can enjoy this journey of life the way I am meant to.

Are you thinking, "Sounds nice, but I don't have time to be present!" Before the retreat, I thought that too. I was constantly running out of time for self-care and being present with my family. But I had to call b.s. because I had time. What was really happening was that I was filling my time with all sorts of things that were not serving me. I was not prioritizing what really mattered.

Here's a little tough love. Not being present, not allowing yourself to take care of you is not admirable. There are no trophies for being the most overworked. There are no accolades for being the most stressed out. There are no ribbons for being the one who has the most on her plate. So can you agree to stop believing that being overworked or having the fullest schedule is what makes you most successful?

Let's focus on presence by practicing a mindfulness exercise right now. It's simple and will only take a few minutes. If you can, find a quiet place where you can sit comfortably and close your eyes. Take a deep breath in, and, as you exhale, let go of any tension or stress in your body. Make noise with the release if you need to. Begin to focus on your breath, feeling the sensation of the air moving in and out of your body.

As you breathe, notice any thoughts or emotions that arise, but do not judge them or try to push them away. Simply acknowledge them and return your attention to your breath. If your mind begins to wander, gently bring it back to the present moment by focusing on your breath.

Keep doing this for as long as you feel comfortable. When you are ready to finish, take a few deep breaths in and out, and slowly open your eyes. By focusing on your breath and bringing your attention to the present moment, you can train your mind to be more present and less reactive and cultivate a greater sense of peace and well-being in your daily life.

Table for One

I began to really shift toward a relationship with myself by engaging in activities that I would normally not do alone. I started going to restaurants alone, hiking alone, and even attending some creative classes alone. Do you date yourself? You know, actually take the time out of your busy schedule to connect with the amazing y-o-u? I wasn't very good at that until the past couple of years when I discovered the value of taking care of myself. The biggest reason: I'm a mom. And do you know what most moms are bad at? Self-care. And do you know why? Because moms feel guilty; they have an unspoken expectation to do it all, be it all, and have it all.

I have many times envied other mothers who could take time out for themselves for even the simplest things like getting an uninterrupted pedicure. When I wasn't advocating for my own self-care, I would ridicule those who did. "What is she thinking? I can't believe she leaves her kids with someone else once a week to go to dinner with her girlfriends. Who does she think she is?" Sound familiar?

As I write this, I sit in an empty, secluded cabin in the woods. I'm here for the night on a business trip and, to be honest, I love it! Sure, getting to the cabin in the dark wasn't fun because, you know, monsters in the woods and all. But now that I'm here, tucked inside, I feel safe. Just with me. On my drive here, I called and caught up with dear friends, karaoked to the great Celine Dion, and also went into a full-on daydream that I was Alanis Morissette. *Isn't it ironic ... don't ya think?*

I can't help but think about you—the woman who doesn't believe that you are worth the long drive to sing about your lovely lady lumps. I mean, aren't you G-L-A-M-O-R-O-U-S? Aren't you worth it? (Insert Fergie dance moves here!)

I'm here to tell you yes, yes you are. You are worth the long drive. You are worth taking time to fall in love with yourself. And there are so many different ways you can do this. Yoga, meditation, pedicures, massages, rocking in a hammock in the park, etc. The fact is, you're worth it! I've been fortunate enough to travel and spend time alone with myself. Even though the current trip I'm on is for business, I choose to take advantage of the opportunity and really enjoy the time to be with lil' ol' me! I had dinner with myself, enjoyed my book (and steak), and now I'm cuddled up next to a warm fire with a glass of wine and my computer.

Whatever it is that sparks fire in you … Whatever it is that helps you connect with your inner self, just do it already!

Nurturing

You know how to nurture others as a wife, a mother, and a friend. But an integral part of being self*ISH* is nurturing yourself. You're never really taught to properly do so; in fact, you might even have to undo the teaching that nurturing yourself is self-centered and uncaring. But, again, you must put on your oxygen mask first because it, literally and figuratively, keeps you alive and makes you better in every other area of life. Your children thrive when they are nurtured. Have you forgotten that you were once a child and that many parts of you still are? Have you abandoned yourself in the pursuit of maturity and forgotten how important nurturing is to your own well-being?

Just a few months ago, I was lucky enough to host and witness a group of women spending an entire day nurturing themselves at my healing event. Along with four other coaches, I helped these women nurture themselves through meditation, breathwork, journaling, and sound therapy. Throughout the day, I saw women step into a higher version of themselves. One woman began the workshop at the end of her rope. She shared that she felt overwhelmed and stressed, like she was on the brink of giving up. After just one day of nurturing, she felt alive again. It wasn't because we coaches were magic workers; it was because she made a decision to step away from all of the things that were causing her negative feelings. She got distance from her stressors so she could gain perspective. She nurtured her inner child who wasn't getting any attention, love, or support.

Nurture yourself by taking care of your physical, mental, and emotional health. My husband, a twenty-year retired veteran, now travels the world saving people from natural and man-made disasters. On his return from one particular mission, he was exhausted physically, spiritually, and emotionally. One of our friends offered him some encouragement: "Rest is holy. Get some." A simple yet profound statement—permission to rest. Ideas of rest are all different. For me, rest can come from putting all of my electronics away and taking a walk or getting in a warm bath. Maybe rest for you is just simplifying your life. Prioritize it by setting boundaries.

Setting boundaries, in general, is a great way to nurture yourself because healthy boundaries keep your energy in alignment with the life that you want. Learn to say "no" when you need to, and prioritize your own needs.

Spend time in joy! Joy is powerful energy. When you feel joy, you feel a sense of gratitude and appreciation for the moment you are in. You feel warmth in your heart—pure bliss! For me, joy is singing and dancing. What makes you feel joyful? Maybe it's connecting with others or cultivating positive friendships. Maybe you find it in solitude and a time of reflection and being present with yourself. Whatever it may be, spend more time in joy.

Remember, nurturing yourself is not selfish, it's self*ISH*. It's an important part of self-care and living a more fulfilling life. Be sure that you're making this and yourself a priority!

Celebration

Celebrating yourself is also a very important part of self-care and self-love. It increases your self-confidence, your self-worth, and your overall well-being. Celebrating myself took a lot of practice. I would accomplish something and then immediately move on to the next thing on my to-do list without stopping to look at how far I had come or acknowledge what I had pulled off against the odds. How could I feel good and hold my head up high if I didn't acknowledge, let alone celebrate, my accomplishments?

How do you celebrate when you complete something on your to-do list? Do you celebrate it or move on to the next thing? Practice being present in the moments that matter in your life, the moments when you can survey how far you have come and appreciate your learning and growth. Start by treating yourself, whether it's to a favorite meal, a spa day, a purchase that you've been eyeing, or even an afternoon nap. These practices will bring about the kind of emotions that make you feel grateful and loved. Living in a space of gratitude shifts your focus to more positivity, which creates a healthier mindset and brings about more to be grateful for! It's a beautiful cycle.

As you move through all of these growth opportunities, reflect on the progress that you've made. You might feel like you're still stuck for the simple reason that you haven't taken the time to reflect on your growth. It's easy to get caught in the trap of feeling as though you can't celebrate yourself until you've made it, but every single step is worth celebrating! Through celebrations, you surround yourself with positivity and people that uplift and inspire you.

Remember, celebrating yourself is not about being self-centered or bragging; it's about acknowledging and honoring yourself because you are worthy and deserving. It's important to be intentional when celebrating yourself. Add the physical feeling to the thought, and feel that pride into reality. It has to move you on an emotional level, or it's not worth doing. Make sure you celebrate in ways that feel authentic and meaningful for you.

In what authentic ways can you celebrate your accomplishments?

Draw on things that make you feel happy, joyful, and excited!

_____

_____

_____

_____

_____

_____

CHAPTER 8
Alignment

To be in alignment means to be one with your dreams. It's a partnership. If you are not in alignment, you feel stuck, lost in life, or like you're merely existing. You struggle to find your purpose and lack motivation to look for it out of fear that you may not have one. Being out of alignment is being out of sync with purpose. But how can you align with purpose if you don't even know what your purpose is?

Feeling out of alignment is common among military spouses. Not only was alignment of purpose difficult for me as a military wife, it was for all of the wives around me as well. The few times I met a military wife who was an entrepreneur, chasing her dreams, and making stuff happen, I would think, "How does she do that? Why can't I?" Instead, I just had an overwhelming feeling of *stuck-ness*. I felt like the desires of my heart didn't meet the purpose that the outside world expected. And then I felt guilty. While my then-husband was deployed to serve my country and protect my freedoms, my purpose should have been to selflessly serve alongside him. Even if it meant putting my dreams and hopes aside. Or at least that's what I thought …

One of the greatest self-inflicted obstacles to your dreams is resistance. I constantly resisted my progress through limiting beliefs, clinging to other people's opinions, lack, and fear.

Unconditional alignment is the key to beating these obstacles. It's the forward movement even when things get in the way. How many times have you witnessed a child trip when they're running but get up as if nothing had happened and continue to play? The resistance is the fall, but unconditional alignment is the active moving forward despite setbacks. As a child, you didn't even know that you were doing it. I often hear people say, "To have the naïvety of a child would be such a gift." As you grow up, you compromise this naïve mindset—this unconditional alignment—based on experiences in your upbringing. You might not even realize how much you've denied alignment until you end up in a place where you feel stuck.

To learn alignment, think of it as any other trade or skill that you're trying to master. You learn as you go, and, therefore, you grow.

Allowance > Resistance

The two main components of focusing on alignment are allowance and resistance. The best thing that you can do is to open up the door to allowance.

To be in a state of allowance means that you are going with the flow. It's organic … the path of least resistance. It's a continuous practice of being in harmony with yourself and your external environment. Imagine you've been working on a project or doing an activity that you're really passionate about. It's something that challenges you enough to keep you engaged but not so much that you feel overwhelmed. You feel a sense of confidence, and your work seems to flow effortlessly. As you work, you all of a sudden realize that several hours have gone by! You didn't even realize what time it was. This is being in a state of allowance. There's no stressful maximum effort, just flow.

Now imagine you're faced with a task toward which you feel resistance. Maybe you're unsure of how to approach it or maybe you're afraid to fail. As you work on it, you might be unfocused, unmotivated, anxious, or stressed. Maybe your body tenses up and feels uncomfortable.

The path of least resistance and greater allowance is to remove yourself from any situation that brings frustration or angst, and try again later. Likewise, when a friend is in a state of frustration, it is not the time to be the voice of reason. Read that again. As a people pleaser, I constantly try to help friends in a period of frustration to see the light, or have a positive attitude, or find the good in the situation. And, nine times out of ten, my good intention is met with resistance. It is not my job to have a hand in someone else's balance of allowance and resistance. I will lose every single time.

All that you control is the resistance that you bring into your own experiences. I have yet to master the art of solving someone else's resistance mindset. Recently, I lost a friend. I thought I was being supportive by showing her all the ways that the negative could be turned into positive, but, unfortunately, it backfired. Not only was this not helpful for her, it caused extra tension between us, and she vented about me to everyone that we knew. When things really blew up, I was confused and hurt. I asked my husband where I went wrong, and he calmly and profoundly replied, "You tried to heal her, and she didn't want you to." Wow. It hit me hard because it's something I've done most of my life. I'm a saver. Well, I used to be a saver. I've finally learned to just worry about and focus on my own growth and healing instead of forcing it on others who aren't yet ready for that journey.

A Better-Feeling Thought

Resistance = feeling bad.
Alignment = feeling good.

That's the simplest way that I can put it. How do you feel right now? If you feel bad, perhaps you are in a state of resistance. Perhaps you are in a cycle of feeling bad, where it seems like nothing ever goes your way. Though this pattern is self-defeating, it can be comfortable if you grew up thinking that life was always going to be hard. This is where you have to get real with yourself and take an inventory on where your energy has been focused.

Do you find yourself complaining a lot? Are you argumentative? Are you carrying around negative energy or blame for a situation over which you had no control? These are all forms of resistance. By remaining in a state of resistance, you continue to bring resistant experiences into your life. Think about a time where you woke up late for work ... you rushed around the house ... you stressed out because you knew that you were going to get stuck in traffic ... you rushed to your closet to pick out your outfit ... and you stubbed your toe on the edge of your bed. You thought, "Why does this always happen to me!?"

Your day snowballs into negative after negative, and it feels impossible to turn it around. Picture this: Your car is on top of a hill, and, all of a sudden, it starts to slowly roll down. If you're at the top of the hill, you can stop it quickly before it picks up momentum. However, if you're halfway down the hill, it's much more difficult to stop it from heading toward certain disaster. The car is like your thoughts. If you're aware of them, you can catch them while they are still at the top. But if you live "halfway down the hill," it's a lot more difficult to chase after them once they have gained momentum.

A better-feeling thought is one that shifts your mindset to a more empowering perspective. It makes you feel good, inspired, and motivated. This is truly a practice. It takes diligence and consistency and will be a work in progress. But once you get into the habit, you'll start doing it naturally.

First, tune into your thoughts and emotions throughout the day. When you notice any feelings of anxiety, negativity, or overwhelm, take a deep breath and ask yourself what thoughts and beliefs are contributing to those feelings. Once you learn to identify those, try to challenge them and ask questions. For example, let's say you feel not good enough. Try to think of times where you have achieved something that you're really proud of! Or, if you're feeling overwhelmed by a big project, break it down into smaller steps that you can take one at a time. Overall, you want to focus on the present moments and the things that you're grateful for in your life. By leaning on that sense of gratitude and appreciation, you shift your mindset toward a positive perspective, and you feel more inspired to take action toward your goals.

Ditching the Hustle

There's no doubt that there's a shift in what mainstream society considers to be success. Success used to mean you had a really impressive résumé, a fancy title at some big-wig corporation, and/or an impressive, elite car. Can you say a resounding "hallelujah" to the fact that this is changing?! They're no longer giving out medals for being overworked and having a stressful schedule. There is no longer any glory in burning out. Nowadays, success is measured more by your emotional intelligence and an awareness of yourself and your personal growth and development.

So are you ready to ditch the hustle? You're not winning by putting yourself last! You're undermining everything that you have already achieved and everything you still want to achieve. You're not a good mom. You're not a good wife. You're not a good business woman when you're unhealthy. When you're stressed, when your nervous system is in overdrive, you are not okay. You are self-sabotaging. You want so desperately to feel good. And yet, you're continuing to set yourself up for failure. This is where resentment comes from. You don't feel resentment when you're well rested, have a nourished soul, or are practicing self-care.

When you're whole and nourished, you can be fully present and show up as a complete person in all of your other roles. You are emotionally regulated, and your nervous system is calm. You're not all stressed out and snappy! You're able to truly be the Divine Queen, the amazing wife, sister, mother, and friend because you show up for yourself first. When you elevate your connection to self, you're modeling to your children and your friends and inspiring others to do the same. Don't be the pot calling the kettle black.

Set up a mental and physical routine that's healthy. Accept that you can have everything, just not all at the same time! Multitasking is a lie sold to profit from overworked people who feel guilty for "not having it all." You're able to do far more of what you desire, far more comprehensively and meaningfully, when your cup is full. "But my kids need me!" You're right! They need a healthy, less-stressed parent who is in touch with themselves and doesn't parent from a place of anger, guilt, or shame. They don't need a snappy little Princess who's stressed out and resentful and who has forgotten why she built this life and family in the first place. They need you to be emotionally available, joyful, and loving.

I have a client who struggles with the hustle game. She feels that if she isn't always doing work of some kind, she is inadequate. She learned through example. She had a mother who constantly found her worth and success around *doing*. In turn, she ended up unknowingly creating a belief system in her daughter that unless she was physically doing something at all times, she was not an adequate member of society or a successful mother. Ouch, right? Think of all of the pressure that comes along with that belief system. It's no wonder women are twice as likely to suffer from stress and anxiety than men. Cut out the hustle—it no longer serves you.

Aligned Action

"Okay, Jenna, that's great and all, and I would love to ditch the hustle, but what do I do instead?" Well, I'm glad you asked. I cut the hustle, so I know exactly how to lead you out of it. The tools I use in this book helped me get into aligned action, and they will do the same for you. As discussed earlier in this chapter, you want to make sure you meet your desires with flow, not with resistance. In order to do so, work only when you're productive. You would be shocked at how often you force yourself into tasks that do not yield a positive result simply because you have been taught that if you aren't *doing* something, you're invaluable.

I've always believed that Europeans have the right work ethic. They work for a few hours in the morning, have several hours off midday, and then come back to work for a few more in the afternoon. Americans (and many others around the world) have it all wrong with the straight eight-hour workday. No one, and I mean no one, is productive all eight hours of their workday. The eight-hour workday was created to stop employers from abusing their employees with limitless work for little pay, not because experts thought employees could focus on tasks for that long. In fact, research has shown that employees who are allowed to take regular breaks and time off are actually more productive and focused than those who are forced to work long hours without rest. When you are able to take breaks and recharge your batteries, you are better able to focus and perform better! Can you imagine how much more productive you could be if you worked from a position of performance with intention?

When do you feel most productive? I typically feel most productive later in the evenings (I am not a morning person!). All you morning people absolutely astound me, but I will never be a member of your club (at least not with a chipper sunshine attitude!). Find a time that works best for you. Stop forcing. Stop trying to fit the square peg through the round hole. It is a complete waste of your precious resources!

That said, when practicing aligned action, be sure to give yourself some grace if it doesn't all go according to plan. The best way to move through those moments of frustration is to take a step back. Walk away from the task in front of you, and come back to it later. Believe it or not, your *subconscious* mind is constantly problem solving. When you take a break from actively trying to hammer out a problem, your brain continues to work on it, making new connections and finding insights that can lead to creative breakthroughs and solutions. Trust in the power of your subconscious mind to work on the problem, and allow yourself the time and space to let the solution emerge.

The more you force it, the more resistance you create around it, which has a negative chemical and energetic effect on your body. When you feel stress and frustration, your brain releases the stress hormones cortisol and adrenaline. This makes it harder for your subconscious to focus on problem solving because your brain is fixated on the problem, not the solution.

Practicing aligned action is part of setting boundaries around your productivity. You are your own individual. Your job is not who you are; it is what you do. Are you able to see the difference between the two? Or have you created your identity around your work? Are you consumed by your job? Have you lost sight of who you really are? This comes at a very high cost to you and the people around you. It is not a healthy state of being. Living in a state of resistance is toxic for your mind and body. It causes chronic stress, which triggers inflammation that has been proven to be the root of many preventable diseases.

You will not accomplish what you're trying to accomplish from this place, so trust in the process of trying to align yourself with action, and live from a place of surrender and flow. Trust in the present, and trust in the knowing that, as you stay aligned with your vision, you will get to the finish line!

CHAPTER 9
Fact or Feeling

In order to know where you're going, you have to know why you're pushing forward. Coaches have many different "why" exercises, but they all share one common conclusion: Your why needs to be deep inside you. It's what will wake you up each day with the motivation and desire to keep moving forward even when it gets hard.

Is your "why" deep enough?
Is your "why" by design?

Often, it's hard to understand your "why." The reason you may struggle to find your "why" is because your body is stuck in a past emotion that is blocking you.

Emotions and beliefs that you hold onto from your past are what continue to be your future reality. When you believe in something so deeply that you physically *feel* into that belief, it creates your future. A belief is just a thought that you think over and over again. Essentially, your focus on an event from the past is keeping that event in your energetic momentum for similar future experiences. The only way that you can move forward toward the life you want is to change your thoughts *and* feelings simultaneously. The first place the resistance starts is in your mind, with your thoughts and your corresponding feelings.

Why is it that the things that are the best for you are the hardest to implement? Because of comfort. When you make a change, such as losing weight, getting sober, or adding meditation to your morning routine, your body thinks, "This feels different and uncomfortable! I really don't like this, please stop." Over your lifetime, you created these neuropathways to protect you physically and emotionally. Thankfully, scientists and thinkers are learning all about neuroplasticity—the ability to reprogram the brain for new and different beliefs! When you engage in new experiences or learn new skills, your brain forms new synapses between neurons, allowing you to better process and retain information. This process of neuroplasticity is at the heart of your ability to adapt to new situations and challenges, allowing you to change and grow. But it requires commitment to push through the discomfort and create new neural pathways that become the changes you want to see in your life.

When I first decided to do the 75 HARD Challenge, a "transformative mental toughness program," man oh man. It was as though my body was yelling, "Please stop, this is stupid! I don't want to do this. Why would you put me through this?" By day sixty-one, I had made my body aware of the new program that we were following. It was through consistency of action that I communicated the new signal to my subconscious: We are making a change. Did that mean that I wouldn't wake up one day and think, "I'm out!" Absolutely not! In fact, throughout the majority of the fifties, I kept trying to justify quitting. I was tired. I told myself that I was missing out on opportunities, rather than seeing the opportunity I was already undertaking. But when I reminded myself of the real reason I was doing it, I didn't want to quit. I reminded myself of the reality that the past sixty-one days had, arguably, been the period of the most exponential growth that I'd had in my personal life for years! I finally overcame the excuses not to follow my dreams. I overcame the lies from society that my role was to play small. I overcame them so I could pursue what I know I was meant to do, which is to help women like you!

What is it that holds you back? Maybe it's a bad habit, or society telling you that you need the corporate job that's sucking the life out of you, or a relationship that has you compromising your values. Whatever it is, you need to identify it so that you can let it go. *Awareness creates change.*

Dr. Joe Dispenza, a leader in mind-body connection work, says that beliefs, the thoughts that you have on a regular basis, are nothing but a record of the past. He also teaches that over half of your beliefs about the past aren't even true! They are embellishments and stories that you have created from the conclusions you have drawn from your experiences. They are usually oversimplified and limiting.

Do you feel stuck? Maybe you've been following the same schedule, working at the same time, going through the same daily program for years—a creature of habit and rigidity. Do you present challenges to yourself and your brain on a daily basis? Or are you always looking for the path of least resistance, which inevitably is the path of most resistance—resistance to change?

As you learn these tools, it is critical that you understand that reading about them is not enough. Even doing the action steps for one week is not enough. You need to make a commitment to change, and do whatever it takes to get there.

What does it usually take before people actually change? Pain. The pain of staying the same has to outweigh the pain of change. I hit this place right before my divorce. I remember watching so many friends of mine level up and excel in life, and I just felt stuck. I was stuck in the belief that my only job on this Earth was to be a supportive military spouse who stayed home with her children, took care of the house, and tried her hand at a multilevel marketing business. And, yes, I was really good at being a spouse and a mother and a silent supporter, but I essentially dissolved into my then-husband. I thrived in the role, until I didn't. I actually lost myself in that role. I woke up one day knowing that I was not living the life that I was created for. I knew that I was created for more. I knew that I wanted more.

I was ready for change.

Are you? Or are you stuck in the past?

When you experience strong emotions, such as joy, fear, or excitement, your brain releases hormones and neurotransmitters that help to cement that memory. Everything that you have an emotional reaction to shapes the way that you experience the world around you. When you recall good-feeling memories, such as your wedding, the birth of your child, or the first time you successfully recreated your grandmother's famous cookie recipe, it likely brings up the same physical feeling that you had when the moment was happening. If it was a really intense emotional experience, you're likely to remember it for longer.

This mind-body connection happens for memories that are traumatic as well and explains why people get stuck. When people ask why you are the way that you are, your response might rely on this event or that incident that happened twenty years before. You're still living in that emotion; therefore, you have created a personality around it, which shows up in your day-to-day life. You take these past experiences and shape them into your beliefs, and your beliefs shape your reality.

But undoing and redoing these beliefs is possible through salience. In neuroscience, salience is the property that makes something stand out. As you practice something new and different, it becomes more salient for you. Essentially, it's a light switch in your brain that allows you to switch from your habitual patterns to a more conscious awareness around how you feel to create a new, more positive response.

Belief

There's a way to get off the hamster wheel of negative emotions. And it has to do with beliefs—patterns that you repeat until they become true. What you have experienced in your lifetime becomes your present reality. The past creates the present and projects into the future. Around and around goes the wheel. Many of your day-to-day beliefs no longer serve you. So why is it that you can't let them go and create new ones?

The short answer is that you don't even realize that you're carrying those beliefs. They are so deeply rooted that you assume the way you see the world is accurate. You may feel like nothing good ever works out for you or that you are not powerful or capable enough to be successful. You may feel shame for being a failure. But it's these outdated beliefs, these stories that you've made up along the way—these untruths—that underlie such negative feelings.

Once you understand that you're evoking feelings based on old, tired, immature, and inaccurate patterns, you can practice substituting in new more realistic, mature thoughts. Easier said than done, but you now have the tools to achieve it!

Let's say that you have something really fun and exciting coming up. Maybe it's a date, or a big presentation, or an interview at the company of your dreams. As you think about it, you feel a positive sensation rise up in your body. You might physically feel the excitement and joy from it before it ever even happens. This is exactly how you "feel into it." Then, you'll have an incredible experience because you embraced and leaned into the positive emotions in advance and manifested that positive experience!

But the same goes for negative feelings. If you allow fear and anxiety to take control before an event or experience, you automatically invite that vibrational feeling into your event or experience. And that will cause you to subliminally focus on negative feelings rather than positive ones.

I was helping a client walk through some past trauma around losing weight. During our time together, we uncovered that the reason she had trouble losing weight was because she was frequently binge eating. We discovered that, as a little girl, her family suffered from food scarcity. She recalled a single experience of babysitting for a wealthy family that had tons of food in their pantry. As it got closer to the end of her shift, she started eating as much of that food as possible. In that moment, she created a belief that if she didn't eat as much as she could, she might not get another chance. At the time of this revelation, she was sixty-two years old! She had lived fifty years and accumulated negative experience after negative experience around food and her body based on an outdated scarcity mindset. At every meal, she unconsciously placated her belief that if she did not eat as much as possible, she may never eat again. That belief was very real to her, just like your beliefs are very real to you.

Your internal perception has an enormous impact on how you perceive the outside world. And you have the power to shift your internal perception toward more positivity and growth. Practicing mindfulness is the first step. Mindfulness is paying attention to your thoughts, feelings, and physical sensations in any present moment without judgment. Practicing regular mindfulness makes you more aware of those internal perceptions.

Once you are aware of your internal perceptions, you can get curious about the negative beliefs and assumptions that you hold about yourself. When you are able to identify them and approach them with curiosity, you can then dig into the truth around them. One question that I like to ask myself is, "What is true?" Just taking a step back to ask that question helps ground me and bring me back to the present and to my controllables.

Creating a new reality means that you need to project a vision onto the future that you hope for. You must remove all of the mental blocks and negativity that have been holding you back.

Limiting beliefs ultimately hold you back from reaching your full potential and achieving your goals. I've struggled most of my life with the limiting belief that I'm not intelligent enough to make an impact. Even as I wrote this book, I could feel it trying to poke its little head up to say, "Stop writing! No one cares! You don't have what it takes!" But you're here, so that limiting belief was wrong!

Every single one of the following beliefs have been real for me and many women with whom I've worked:

> *"I'm not good enough."* Wowhew. Did you feel that? This one hits deep for many women. It can manifest in different ways, such as, "I'm not smart enough" or "I'm not talented enough." This limiting belief is responsible for you not wanting to step out of your comfort zone and try new things.

> "I don't deserve success." Self-sabotage alert!!! This one can single-handedly prevent you from taking action. It can cause you to sit in a state of procrastination and leave you feeling like you're stuck in a rut. Talk about imposter syndrome.

> One of the most powerful limiting beliefs that women struggle with, especially when you are getting divorced or attempting a career change, is, "I'm too old/young." In reality, age is *never* a limiting factor, but you make it one when you compare

yourself to other women. I struggled with this limiting belief when I first started building my business after being a stay-at-home mom for many years. I felt like I was too late to the game and felt jealous of other women who had, what I perceived at the time, the luxury of starting their careers earlier in life. I felt cheated and bitter as I thought about all of the "catching up" I needed to do. I had to shift my mindset so that this belief didn't prevent me from taking action and moving forward.

Desire

If you don't believe in what you're desiring, you will never get what you want.

Everything that is activated in your vibration (your energy) will show up for you immediately. You just have to be open to seeing it. Two years ago, I made a commitment to become wealthy and find abundance. This was really difficult for me because my outlook on money was that if you had a lot of it, you would be perpetually stressed trying to keep it. My parents were raised by Great Depression-era parents, so it was only natural that all of their future generations believed we had to hold onto every penny we made in case of an emergency. As bizarre as it sounds, going into adulthood, I was more comfortable with debt than I was with the thought of having an abundance of money.

But because my heart's desire was to serve others and be a force for good, I realized that I need to change my beliefs around money. I needed more money and a healthier approach to money because then I could help more people!

So I intentionally set that desire, and you know what happened next? I started finding pennies all over the place! Every time I found a penny, I would feel a huge rush of energy through my body. I proclaimed (loudly) that I was attracting money and being taken care of. And I didn't just *say* it, I *felt* it! Sounds silly, right? Only if you don't like money. What does this do for me? It adds another layer to the energy that I'm putting into the world as I proclaim and show gratitude for every single penny that comes my way.

What is your heart's desire? Is it more money? If so, what would more money mean for your life?

_____

_____

_____

_____

_____

_____

Once you're crystal clear on your desires, you send that energy into motion and start calling it into your life. And this is when the real magic happens!

Calling It In

When you call something to yourself, you are *inviting* it in. You are saying to God and to the universe that you are ready to receive everything that you desire. Again, this cannot be something that you fake. It cannot be something that you force. It has to be something that you truly are connected to in your mind, body, and soul.

If you have trouble connecting to it, it's probably not your true desire. Remember, your desires need to spark a positive emotion or feeling within your body. I live by the motto: "If it isn't a heck yes, it's a heck no!" Luckily, you have an inner guidance that will show up. Take time to sit in silence, breathe in slowly and deeply, and ask yourself, "What is my *truest* desire?" It's okay if this takes some time. It's worth pursuing until you find it.

What do you feel is being called to you?

_____

_____

_____

_____

_____

_____

When you call something into your life and say that you are ready for it, you better buckle up because really cool things begin to happen! There are some great prayers that you can pray each day to call in all of your desires. I recommend my clients either write them out in a dry erase marker on their mirror or put them on little Post-it notes around the house. If you saw my house, you would laugh at all the Post-it notes on every surface!

When you write a prayer, don't just put it on paper ... *say it* out loud, *feel it* as you write it, *proclaim it* as you write it. Get excited as you write it!

> › Opportunities are coming to me now!
> › I am abundant in all areas of my life!
> › I am grateful that I am constantly attracting abundance!
> › Wealth and abundance are natural parts of my life!
> › I respect my abilities and trust them to generate wealth!
> › Today, I am calling in high vibrations, a positive mindset, and all of the abundance!
> › I have the power to step into the highest version of myself anytime I choose to!
> › I attract everything I desire with ease!

You can create statements that are true for your own desires. Be sure that you write down things that inspire you and bring out a feeling of excitement.

Releasing

Now that you're calling all of these incredible things into your life, you need to make space for them to show up. There are distractions, limiting beliefs, and flat-out time-suckers that will take up the space in your life that is meant for the things that you are attracting.

Identify what does not serve you anymore. Take time to reflect on all the things in your life that do not bring you any joy or fulfillment. These can be anything from a relationship to a negative thought pattern. Acknowledge the impact that they have on your life. Realize that the emotion being triggered as you think about the particular thing is the energy that blocks you from attracting what you want into your life. The anxiety and stress that come from those things that no longer serve you prevent you from reaching and achieving your goals.

Making a list isn't enough. You have to decide to let go of what no longer serves you. Only then will you free yourself from its impact.

This decision might make you feel guilty, but that's okay! Practice self-compassion. Be kind to yourself through this process because letting go can be uncomfortable and can cause feelings of sadness and grief. But ask yourself which is more uncomfortable: processing the things that you need to shed in your life or living in a continuous pattern that makes you feel stuck?

I recently worked with a woman who needed to let go of a long-term friendship. She and her friend had been through a lot of life together, but she knew deep down that the friendship was no longer serving her. She struggled with the guilt of seeming "too good" for her friend, but she knew this was out of her control. Remember, no one can control how other people perceive their decisions. It was a very difficult and stressful time while she grieved the loss of the friendship. We were able to walk through it and show love and gratitude for the times that they had together and the things that they learned from each other. Eventually, she was able to release the friendship with love and light.

I recommend seeking support through the releasing experience, whether it be from a friend, a family member, or even a counselor who can walk you through it. A really powerful tool is a forgiveness exercise. I walk you through this in detail at serviceandsoul.com. Just remember that letting go is a process, and it does take time. Be patient with yourself, and be sure to celebrate the small wins along the way.

CHAPTER 10
Purpose-Filled Life

One of the hardest things in life is to find your purpose. I remember the day my husband told me that he had been approached about a job opportunity with an organization that responds to man-made and natural disasters. It meant that he would, once again, be on a deployment schedule. My immediate reaction was a resounding, "Heck no!" I resisted it because I had already lived the life of being second to my spouse's job. And we were finally in a place of "normalcy." My husband was home every night, which allowed space for me to finally chase my dreams and desires. After a lot of discussion, I realized that my mindset was proclaiming that my purpose was more important. After being trained for twenty years at a cost of millions of dollars, he was not feeling fulfilled in this so-called "normal life."

So how could we create a life where we were both living for our purpose? Until that moment, my experience was that only one of us could pursue our purpose while the other took care of the family and home. But I realized that this was an outdated belief based on my early adulthood while being a military spouse. I finally truly understood and believed that there was room for everyone to fulfill their calling.

My husband did end up taking that job, and watching him truly rise into what he was called to do has been such an amazing experience. Because I was able to authentically support him on his path to purpose, I was further inspired to rise into mine—working to support and be a safe place for military and first responder spouses who are ready to stop playing small.

It's time for you to stop playing small.
It's time for you to rise into your purpose and calling.
The world needs you to do that!

How do you even begin to find out your purpose? The first step is to ask what it is that you're passionate about and interested in. What truly excites you? What energizes you? Think about activities, topics, or causes that bring you joy. Pay attention to moments when you feel most alive and engaged.

Let's write them out:

_____

_____

_____

_____

_____

_____

_____

_____

Now take it to the next level. What are your strengths and talents? Consider the skills and abilities that come naturally. What do you excel at and enjoy doing?

_____

_____

_____

_____

_____

What are your values? What matters most to you? Think about the beliefs that guide your life and the causes about which you deeply care.

_____

_____

_____

_____

_____

Remember that finding your purpose is a journey, and it evolves as you grow and learn. Be open to exploring and being curious about things as they come along the way. Hire a coach or join a course that can provide support and guidance. Always keep in mind that this is a continual growth experience. By doing this exercise consistently, you can uncover your unique path and live a life filled with meaning.

Next Steps

"Neurons that fire together, wire together."
- Donald Hebb

In order to make a true change and shift in your life, you have to do new things that are aligned with your vision and desire. What does this really mean? It means that you're going to create new daily habits and thought patterns to help you shift your current momentum and energy.

If you do the same things, go through the same motions, and have the same emotions, you will get stuck in life. The nerve cells in your body store memory and energetically communicate with each other to form your behavior. Think of it as a game of follow the leader. Once one synapsis forms and stores a memory, the rest communicate with each other and fall in line. Over time, that feeling, based on communication (via energy) between your nerve cells, becomes your way of life until you fire the neurons in a different direction. By the time you're, say, thirty-five, if you have not changed those thoughts and patterns, you have told every cell in your body that this is who you are. There's a reason they call it a midlife crisis! It's because you get stuck on autopilot and feel as though you need an overwhelming change or life experience to get out of it. You need something exciting to shake things up. But something material or superficial rarely results in a new, happier version of yourself. Instead, you may end up feeling even more hopeless because it didn't improve your core or create momentum toward a lasting change. Luckily, you now have the knowledge to create real and meaningful change.

Let's list the things (let's call them "threats") that currently hold you back from discovering your "why."

_____

_____

_____

_____

_____

Now write down the things that you feel like you need to implement in your daily life but haven't because they're uncomfortable.

_____

_____

_____

_____

_____

What would it look like if you started doing these things? What would your body feel like day to day if you implemented these tools in your life? (Think about who you're with, where you are, what possessions you have, the people that you encounter, etc.)

_____

_____

_____

When you wrote these down, did you get an overall perspective on what can shift? If it didn't create clarity for you, I recommend taking more time to ask these curiosity questions and really allow your inner being to open up and express itself so that you can truly make what you desire come to life.

Hope

Once you start shifting these limiting beliefs and creating your new reality, you will have a new sense of hope for your future. Hope is different for everybody—what it looks like for me may be different for you.

Hope is the driving force that keeps you moving forward. It's the belief that things will change and get better. It's easy to feel like there's nothing to be hopeful for when things are going wrong; but all it takes is a moment for your whole life to change. Anything is possible. Without hope, you'll feel like there's no point in even trying. Not only does hope help you persevere, it also reduces stress, anxiety, and depression, and it increases your overall sense of well-being.

I remember when my life truly began to feel more hopeful. When I was going through all of the pain of my divorce, I felt a knowing deep inside of me that there was a rainbow on the other side of the storm. It was a "fake it 'til you make it" moment. You know the kind where you really don't have much to lose, but you have hope? And I remember forcing myself to believe that everything was going to be okay.

One night, after a few months of being in our new place, my oldest son yelled at me through his pain: "How can you be so happy right now?! Look around! Our family is falling apart, and I don't understand how you can still have a smile on your face!" He didn't know it at the time but I felt the Little Girl inside of me wanting to scream, "Don't you think I know that?!" I wanted to throw my hands up in defeat. But my Queen was making her debut, and her opening act was one of hopefulness that this change had a purpose. Was it easy for me to find hopefulness? No. It was really hard! But I knew that I didn't have any other choice if I wanted to make it out on a brighter side. I had to decide on hope not only for myself, but also as an example for my children.

There are several ways to achieve a hopeful mindset. Reflecting on past times where I overcame challenges or achieved something meaningful helps me. Try it. Reflect on your past successes to remind you of what you're capable of and how resilient you truly are. Also, practice gratitude. Take inventory on anything and everything that you are grateful for big or small—there's always something! Prioritize things that bring you joy, relaxation, and fulfillment. Challenge any negative, inaccurate thoughts, and replace them with positive, realistic thoughts. Most importantly, seek out positive and supportive relationships. Surround yourself with people who believe in you and your potential!

Connection

You were born with a desire for connection. From the minute you were held after birth, your nervous system created the feel-good hormones around connection. When you have positive social interactions, your brain releases chemicals that promote feelings of happiness and well-being, including oxytocin, "the love hormone."

When I feel a loss of connection to myself or an outside relationship, I really struggle to push through moments of resistant thoughts and feelings. However, if I've been working on myself and focusing on my connection to others in my support system, I feel like I could conquer anything! The power of connection not only boosts your mood, but gives you a sense of belonging while lowering rates of depression and anxiety, as well as improving your physical health.

This is why it is so important that you surround yourself with people that you want to be like. When you're around such like-minded people, you feel motivated and excited for life! It's a feeling of belonging, of being understood, appreciated, and valued by others. It is a feeling of being seen and heard and knowing you are part of something bigger than yourself, that you are not alone. When you're connected, you're less lonely and isolated, and you feel more supported in everything that you do. You are able to share happiness and sadness and receive love and encouragement.

Think about a time when you felt unconditional love. If you had a tougher childhood, maybe it was from a teacher or the mother of a close friend. Remember how it felt to be supported? To know that someone could really see you? Where do you lack that feeling in your life right now? Who do you wish saw the real you? If you struggle with feeling like you're in the shadows, you need to seek out connection.

First, reflect on your core values and what truly matters to you. Then, find an aligned community.

Who can you reach out to? Maybe it's a networking group or people who share your hobby. Volunteering for a cause that you care about can help you create a sense of purpose and connection.

What type of local groups could you join? Seek out new experiences by stepping outside of your comfort zone to meet like-minded individuals and create opportunities for meaningful connections.

Have you overlooked a connection that you already have? Maybe there is an old friend that you could reconnect with.

To further strengthen connections, you can also, right now, make an effort to be more present with others. Show genuine interest in their lives by actively listening. Give your full attention and respond with empathy and understanding. Active listening fosters deeper connections and helps others feel heard and valued.

Connection doesn't benefit just you; it also benefits others. It's a two-way street. When you show up for other people with support and empathy, you'll receive that in return. Remember, the energy that you put out correlates with what you get back. Once you unconditionally support others, imagine how many people will give that back to you.

CHAPTER 11
Talking Body

*"Neuroscience research shows that the only way we can change
the way we feel is by becoming aware of our inner experience and
learning to befriend what is going inside ourselves."*
- Bessel van der Kolk

I'll never forget the first time I realized my body was talking to me.
I was doing restorative yoga at a retreat. We were guided into child's
pose, a simple yet comforting posture, where you kneel down, sit
back on your heels, and fold your upper body forward allowing
your forehead to rest on the mat or the floor. It's like gently hugging
yourself so that you calmly focus on your breath and relax into the
floor that's supporting you. So I was in child's pose, aligning my
chakras, and trying to look out of my third eye when, all of a sudden, I
felt an unexpected urge that completely caught me off guard.
Before I could shove it down, I was crying. The tears had come out of
nowhere! I didn't enter the yoga practice feeling sad or overwhelmed.
But the crying felt so natural that I let it flow. I just went with it.

Since I had recently read Bessel van der Kolk's book, *The Body Keeps
the Score: Brain, Mind, and Body in the Healing of Trauma*, I was

super curious as to what was coming up for me ... what I could have possibly been holding in my body to cause such a dramatic experience. I learned that child's pose, specifically, engages the hips, which store feelings of abandonment. It clicked! Though I always believed that abandonment trauma was only caused by physical or emotional neglect as a child, adults also can experience it even if someone isn't intentionally abandoning them. I was finally able to acknowledge the abandonment trauma that I experienced as a military spouse. My then-husband was in a special operations unit and could deploy anytime, any day. And even if he wasn't deployed, he was away training somewhere else in the world. His duty was to always answer the military's call, not my call. Was he intentionally abandoning me? Not at all! Was I still creating pathways of abandonment each time I was left alone to fend for myself? Turns out, I was.

This is why it matters that you show up for yourself and learn how to listen to your body and what its physical manifestations might be telling you. Your body is an intelligent creation that alerts you when something is physically or energetically offline. Think about it as having your check engine light come on to let you know that there is something physically or emotionally needing attention. I am now able to use this information from my body to focus on my healing so that I can peacefully move through that part of my resistance with ease.

Have you ever had an emotional response to a physical movement? Write about it. How did it show up for you?

_____

_____

How can you use this experience for growth?

_____

_____

_____

_____

_____

_____

Listening to Your Body

Whether you currently know how to listen to it or not, your body is always communicating with you. If you struggle with conditions like autoimmune disease and unexplained weight gain, you may have something completely unrelated going on within you. The natural response is to assess what you're eating or what your level of activity is, but those symptoms often are masking underlying emotional trauma. Sadly, you may not know how to listen.

Your body can communicate through subtle physical sensations like having butterflies in your stomach when you're on a first date or having a racing heart when you're about to do something that scares you. The signal that many women find difficult to decipher is intuition. How often have you questioned that inner "gut feeling" and ignored it? If a specific memory came to mind, how did that situation work out for you? Learn from that experience for when you sense it in the future.

Your body also signals you through your energy level. You may have been raised to push through pain or to show up even if you didn't feel like it. But, sometimes, you just need rest! And that's okay! If you feel tired or sluggish, it could be a reaction to a physical trigger like lack of sleep or an emotional or mental stressor. Your body might be telling you that you need to take better care of your health.

One of the greatest things I ever learned was how much the gut affects the brain. In fact, many researchers call the gut "the second brain" because it has so many complex systems of neurons and neurotransmitters that are responsible for not only controlling your digestion, but also for sending and receiving signals to and from your brain through your vagus nerve (the longest nerve in your body). This system is referred to as the enteric nervous system; it is responsible for triggering large emotional responses. "For decades, researchers and doctors thought that anxiety and depression contributed to these types of gut problems. But our studies and others show that it may also be the other way around," explains Dr. Jay Pasricha, director of the Johns Hopkins Center for Neurogastroenterology. Essentially, there is a two-way connection between your gut and your brain that plays a critical role in regulating your emotions.

That feeling of butterflies you get when you feel excited or nervous is your vagus nerve firing, telling you something. The same goes for when your heart races or you get an upset stomach when you feel anxious. This theory of a connection between gut and brain via the vagus nerve is known as the polyvagal theory and explains how your *emotions* physically travel up and down your body.

The impact of the enteric nervous system is just one way in which your body talks to you. It is imperative to listen, lest you struggle with some form of dis-ease.

Dis-ease

Do you feel like you have little control over diseases and diagnosed medical conditions—as though your physical self is separate from your mental/emotional self? Your health actually can be affected by your thoughts and feelings. While it's not a direct cause, the indirect ramifications of negativity can, ultimately, trigger disease. Chronic stress, for example, increases inflammation in your body, which, in turn, impairs your immune system, which then can cause you to feel sluggish and unmotivated. When you live in a chronic state of negativity, you catalyze physical changes in your body, which can become disease.

Are you one of the astounding numbers of women who walk around in an uncomfortable physical state and have no idea that you can feel better just by changing the way you view the world? You already know that practicing positive emotions can have a positive impact on mental health like reducing anxiety and depression. But positivity also has been scientifically linked to better physical health! Practicing positive emotions lowers levels of inflammation; it also reduces the risk of chronic diseases like heart disease and diabetes.

Many people have reversed disease using the power of their thoughts. One of the most popular success stories is that of Joe Dispenza, someone who I listen to and learn from on a regular basis. Back in the 1980s, Joe was involved in a serious bicycle accident that resulted in multiple fractures in his vertebrae. Doctors said that he would need surgery to repair the damage and would likely face a lifetime of chronic pain and limited mobility. As a chiropractor, he was not willing to accept this as his reality. He knew that there was a better way based on his studies of visualization and the fields of neuroscience and quantum physics. He researched the mind-body connection and the power of the mind to heal the body. Throughout the time of his injury and recovery, he practiced visualization and meditation techniques to reprogram the thoughts around his injury and his ability to heal. He would sit and imagine his vertebrae healing bone by bone. This took him a very long time, but, ultimately, he was able to make a full recovery without surgery and avoided a lifetime of both chronic pain and limited mobility. Now he helps others harness the same power.

I encourage you to study the mind-body connection and learn how to take inventory on what you're feeling physically and emotionally. Take the time to sit with yourself to ask the questions, and be still enough to hear the answers.

Energy

Everything in your life is linked to your nervous system and your emotions. You create certain strategies of thinking and patterns of behavior while growing up in order to protect yourself and stay safe. These coping mechanisms then determine how you react and respond to what happens around you even as an adult. In order to heal physically and emotionally, you need to create new systems to interrupt those patterns that stop you from creating new neural pathways.

As Tony Robbins put it, "Lots of people know what to do, but they don't do what they know." When I heard that for the first time, its truth stopped me in my tracks. Think about how many times you've heard someone say, "I know I'd feel better if I cut out all of the caffeine, but it's just so hard!" or "I know if I could set aside ten minutes a day to organize my tasks, I could drastically increase my daily productivity." You hear, and say, similar things, but do you actually take that action to create what you desire?!

I realized that in order to truly achieve all that I desire, I need to have a deep connection with the outcome I am working toward. I've written a lot about energy in this book and the importance of creating positive energy around desires, but I want to go a little more in depth about this. Have you ever noticed how your energy shifts around the things you truly desire? When you see someone you love, do you feel almost as though you're buzzing? It's often a physical sensation that you can feel rising up from your core. It's a physical feeling of pure joy and excitement! That is the type of energy that you want to hold onto because it helps you stay motivated and committed. Think about it. Why would you spend any time or energy on things that don't make you light up inside? Usually, you actively try to avoid that energy because it doesn't feel good.

Of course, there will be times that you don't feel positive energy around your dreams. You'll encounter roadblocks and circumstances that discourage you and make you feel less than. That's when you have to ensure that you don't get caught up in those negative emotions of fear, doubt, or frustration because they can drain your energy and make it harder for you to stay motivated. Whenever I feel like I am forcing creativity around something that I'm passionate about, I take a break and refocus on why I'm passionate about it in the first place. This always helps me find joy again!

If you find yourself in a moment where you're feeling frustrated or negative, stop. I don't mean stop feeling that way, I mean stop what you're doing. Walk away, take a step back, and regroup. A step back might even be a full day or two, and that's totally okay. What's important is to notice yourself in that negative space and not get caught up in that momentum. When you feel inspired to try again, be aware that you are in alignment with the positive energy.

Movement

Movement is one of the most impactful yet least utilized tools to change and improve how you feel. There are the obvious benefits, such as improving your energy levels and your mood, but it goes so much deeper than that. When you feel good, you are more likely to stay motivated to take action. Exercise releases endorphins, which are natural, feel-good chemicals that help reduce stress, anxiety, and depression.

I think something that holds a lot of people back from exercise and movement is the notion that, in order for it to count, you have to go to a gym or do something extremely strenuous. This is not true. Movement comes in so many different avenues, such as dance, stretching, and yes ... even sex!

With just thirty minutes of movement each day, you can improve your overall health and well-being and feel stronger, with the physical and mental energy to pursue your desires. You might read this and think, "This is great; I'm going to enroll in a challenge." Let me talk about challenges, particularly the extreme challenges—the cold plunges, the 75 HARD, the Whole30-type challenges. These are appealing because they seem like a quick fix; something that's going to jolt your nervous system and make you feel alive again. I have done so ... many ... challenges! I've done the bodybuilding shows, the marathons, the fit challenges ... Hell, I even created a few challenges during my coaching days. From a marketing standpoint, it is a genius idea because people buy challenges time and time again.

Why might you choose these sorts of challenges over and over? Because you're not healing deeply, at your core (yes, hi, I've been there before!). Rather, physical challenges mask your current feelings by making you feel accomplished in the short term and temporarily forget what it is that you ultimately want to feel better about.

There is, physically, nothing wrong with challenges. But I want you to be aware of using them to avoid the healing that you actually need. You might participate in these sorts of challenges to find validation and self-worth. Yet, despite having accomplished these great things, you still feel unfulfilled. Why else would you go back for more?

When I was a personal trainer and weight-loss trauma coach, I guided women through their body image trauma by helping them process their past experiences and how these affected their relationships with diet and exercise. Processing these deep-rooted issues is the most powerful healing. Don't hide from the root causes with physical short-term gains. Use movement as a proper tool to lead you past these underlying challenges, not as its own hurdle.

If you remember nothing else from this book, remember this: Getting your body moving each day and making a commitment to that provides a sense of accomplishment and progress. This sends a message to your subconscious: "I can do something and be successful." This boosts your confidence and motivation to continue to pursue your desires in other areas of your life.

Your body deserves to feel good. You deserve to feel good! So take this as a sign that you need to give yourself this gift and get that body moving several days a week in whatever way feels good to you. Your body, mind, and desires will thank you for it!

CHAPTER 12
Go With the Flow

Getting into the flow means that you create momentum for your life without force. You heard that, right? *Without* force. How? Don't tie your happiness to the end result. You must cultivate happiness first! In other words, you need to be happy *now*.

This is the true internal happiness that you need in order to have the courage and moxie to reach your goals. And true happiness comes without external accomplishments. Being in the flow is a mental state that pulls you toward your dreams, all while being happy with exactly where you are and who you are right now.

There's a difference between being in control of the circumstances in your life and being in control of the way that you feel about the circumstances in your life. You can waste all your time and energy trying to control the circumstances themselves, but you will only create resistance and, thus, call forth the roadblocks that keep coming into your experience.

Creating flow should be one of your top priorities when it comes to building your dream life. Think about an athlete who trains their body and their mind. When they are in the flow, they are fully committed to their goals and their dreams.

Being in the flow means inspiration, surrender, and connection to the dreams you desire. Flow is a state of being. It is not forced, it just is. Your body will feel graceful and calm, and your mind will feel peace. Flow brings clarity, harmony, optimal time management, and effortlessness.

In what ways do you feel flow? Maybe it's while you paint, do pottery, dance, or write a book!

Clarity

When you pray over a decision, you probably pray for clarity. The unknown can be daunting and confusing. But you need clarity in your goals and visions because if you don't know where you want to go, how are you going to plan your path to get there?

One of the best ways to find clarity is to ask for it. I know ... mindblowing!

If you struggle with clarity, lean into some questions that can help.

What can bring me happiness right now?

_____

_____

_____

_____

_____

What is distracting my energy?

_____

_____

_____

_____

_____

What have I recently accomplished that I'm proud of?

_____

_____

_____

_____

_____

_____

How did my body feel with this accomplishment?

_____

_____

_____

_____

How do I define success?

_____

_____

_____

_____

What does my ideal life look like? (Who am I with? What am I doing?)

_____

_____

_____

_____

_____

These questions are great prompts to help guide you toward clarity. Write them out. They don't have to be perfect; momentum is key!

When you slow down and take a step back, you find clarity. When you put the phone away and practice mindfulness, you find clarity. Knowing what you want to accomplish makes it easier to make decisions and prioritize your time.

Harmony

Flow also brings peace and harmony. I've talked a lot about the importance of not forcing results. Anything that you try to force will not only feel unnatural, but will also not be sustainable. Happiness is not about more intensity; it's about more surrender and letting go. Living in harmony feels like finding the perfect balance within yourself and the world. You feel confident, peaceful, and content; everything is in perfect alignment. You feel so much true connection to your inner self that the people around you see it within you. Your relationships are more fulfilling because you connect on a much deeper level. All of your thoughts, feelings, and actions are in sync.

Living in harmony doesn't mean that everything is perfect or that you won't face challenges. Harmony doesn't always flow naturally. Often your needs and desires clash with those around you. Life is complicated; conflict arises and throws you off your game. But when those challenges arise, harmony will allow you to move through them with ease, grace, and resilience. It's a continuous journey, so when you recognize harmony in your life, take note of it so that you can internalize it and strengthen it more and more each day.

What are some things that you do to create harmony?

_____

_____

_____

_____

_____

Set an intention today to do more of these activities to kickstart your flow.

Time

I once coached a young woman who felt constantly overworked. She was frustrated because not only was she starting and growing a business, she also had two children and a household to run. Talk about chaos! When you experience chaos, you rely on your survival instincts—fight, flight, or freeze. This causes physical stress in your body, which not only triggers emotional distress, but creates dis-ease. The key to taming such chaos is protecting your *time*. After all, time and harmony work hand in hand. What my client, and countless others, needed to do was to learn how to delegate. What is an hour worth to you? What can you do with your time to create more harmony in your experiences? This particular client hired someone to help run the household duties so that she could focus on getting her business off the ground.

You might be thinking, "That's nice. I don't have enough time to even think about time!" And then you may feel guilty because, as the saying goes, "We all have the same twenty-four hours in a day." But is that really true? A mentor of mine gracefully pointed out that that saying is absolute nonsense! You and I *do not* have the same twenty-four hours in a day that someone like Elon Musk does!

Allow me to explain. While you mathematically have the exact same twenty-four hours in a day, someone like Elon Musk has 2,640,000 hours in a day. How? He delegates to 110,000 employees, who also each have twenty-four hours in a day. Multiply 110,000 employees by twenty-four hours, and he has 2.64 million hours. Do you see where I'm going? The reason why you may struggle with time and the lack of it is because you don't know how to delegate, plan, or weed out the time-suckers that you have in your daily life. Before you start arguing with me that you cannot afford 110,000 employees, I'm going to remind you that your words become your world.

I, too, once had "no money" to hire someone to whom I could delegate. My advice to you is find the money. Ask for it. Believe that it will come to you. It'll feel scary at first, but you will accomplish more with grace and ease when you have someone else to delegate to. This will increase your time and allow you to make the decisions you need to make. As a wife and a mom, it felt uncomfortable for me to think about hiring someone else to help take care of our home. That was *my* job. I was taught that I needed to be able to do that and everything else because that meant I was a superhero, which meant I would "earn" the cape. What a joke! Did you know there are people out there who thoroughly enjoy taking care of a household? Yep. I actually pay someone to do that for me now. And you know what? She makes a living off of it (hello abundance), and she is in her state of flow doing it! She and I do not have the same flow. She is in her state of harmony, which allows me to be in mine.

Effortlessness

The idea of effortlessness can be confusing when used incorrectly. Sitting around and waiting for something to happen for you is not what it means to effortlessly flow through life. To truly be effortless is to take action on the things in your life that you have passion for. These are where you feel flow and effortlessness. But be careful not to get stuck in the mindset that if things get hard while moving toward your dreams that it's not working. No one, and I mean no one, is ever truly able to achieve anything great without putting in serious effort. Think about a woman that you personally know and admire. What have you seen her go through? What trials and tribulations did she have to overcome before she arrived at where she is today? Do you really believe that she achieved all of that without putting in any effort? Of course not! She's likely spent years honing her craft, failing, and pushing herself to be better and to thrive.

So why might you cling to the "easy" notion of effortlessness? Probably because you are taught to believe that you have to do it all perfectly and with ease. And if you can't, you shouldn't bother trying. If you fail, then it's a sign that you weren't meant to do it in the first place. But there's no shame in falling down and getting back up again. It's something that you should be proud to do. It builds resilience, and resilience ensures that you always believe you are capable of achieving your dreams.

Don't misunderstand. You shouldn't overwork and stress yourself to the point where you burn out. Rather, I encourage you to release the stress of perfectionism, and, instead, embrace striving, perseverance, and tenacity. Be proud of any accomplishment, no matter how big or small. What matters is that you continue to move forward.

Degrees of Flow

There are many different types and degrees of flow.

Let's start with the highest degree of flow, which is simply referred to as flow state. When you're in the flow state, you are fully absorbed with the task at hand. You feel good. You feel connected. You feel accomplished. You lose track of time, lost in the pleasure of being. It feels as though nothing else in the world exists. It's a true sense of being present in the moment; a true sense of connection to working toward your goals.

Do you remember the last time you felt this way? You want to try to be connected to the flow state at all times. And you'll feel frustrated when you're not. But feeling frustrated outside of this state is pointless because it's not a state you can be in on demand. It is a matter of being in harmony. The next time you are frustrated when trying to achieve flow, express love and gratitude toward yourself and your ability to do the work, and thank the frustration for showing up at that moment. Expressing gratitude toward setbacks can help you cultivate a sense of humility and openness to feedback. By recognizing that there is always room for improvement, you can remain open to new ideas and approaches and continue to grow and develop your skills.

Next is controlled flow—the medium level of flow. When you're in controlled flow, you are still very engaged in what you are doing, but you're also distracted by other things. It's hard to maintain your focus and stay absorbed due to all the distractions around you. The only way to move from this state to the flow state is to completely remove yourself from distractions that may arise. When you truly desire to be in the flow state, it's important to not multitask or try to fit too many things in your cart. When you try to focus on multiple tasks at once, your attention is divided as you switch back and forth between them. This constant switching is mentally exhausting and leads to increased stress and decreased productivity.

The third level of flow is the boredom, or apathy, stage—the very lowest degree of flow. When you're in this stage, all bets are off. You're frustrated; you're trying to fit a square peg through a round hole and meeting much resistance in the process. You might start talking yourself out of what you are trying to achieve and assume that it was a mistake to believe you could achieve it in the first place. This is when you need to stop what you are doing, take a step back, recognize the familiar critical voice in your head, and know that this is not true. This stage of flow is not a reflection of your abilities or your worth.

To get in tune with flow, focus on finding your flow indicators— what you feel when you're optimally performing. For example, when you're at your highest level of creativity, you'll have a physical reaction in your body. Perhaps it's excitement or momentum. It feels good. It feels natural. It feels like it's coming without any resistance. When you're in that state of feeling, acknowledge it, and call more of it into you.

Now you might be wondering, "How do I even start to discover what my flow is?" First, find an activity that can induce flow. Maybe it's meditation, taking a walk, or listening to an inspirational podcast. These are all ways to rid yourself of the distractions that keep you playing small and making excuses. You're building a personal relationship with yourself.

A flow-based life is all about intentionally slowing down and simplifying. You'll create space for the things that truly matter like spending time with loved ones, pursuing your passions, and taking care of yourself. When you slow down, you become more mindful and intentional about how to spend your time and energy.

When you're in the state of flow, you will call unexpected opportunities into your life. You will know that you're in the flow when your desires come your way with little to no effort. Does this mean that you can sit around and wait for life to happen to you? Absolutely not! It takes work. But you'll achieve a state of flow when you are not creating resistance in your life and can energetically pull in what you desire. This applies not only in personal relationships, but also in business. You will realize, over time, that people are going to meet you where you are. If you're in a state of lack, you will attract other people who are also in lack. If you are in a state of abundance, you will attract people who are also in a state of abundance.

CHAPTER 13
Say Yes!

What if you said yes? Yes to the trip. Yes to the relationship. Yes to the adventure. Yes to writing a book. Yes to starting a business. Yes to the new house. Yes to that new job. How would your life turn out if you focused on faith and not fear? What would it look like to lean into the knowing of your own intuition and guidance system?

When you connect to self and acknowledge and embrace your inner strength, wisdom, and intuition, you learn how to discern between what is faith-based and what is fear-based. Faith is a belief or trust in something or someone; it also can give you a sense of purpose and motivation to push through challenges and pursue your dreams. Fear, on the other hand, is an emotion that is triggered by a perceived threat or danger.

Faith and true belief is understanding how energy works. It's understanding that the feeling must come before the result. It's understanding that your brain thinks the thought and your body feels the feeling, but that they have to act in unison for the desire to manifest into reality. That's where a lot of people get it wrong. You can't simply focus on your affirmations and your mantras and then sit back and wait for the manifestation to happen. It doesn't work that way. The thought/desire must pair with the feeling that it's already happened in order to energetically set what you desire into motion.

Distraction

Distraction is anything that prevents you from giving your full attention to something else.

And there are SO … MANY … DISTRACTIONS!

Distractions can come in all shapes and sizes. I used to pull out my phone at every red light because I was concerned that something had to have happened in the thirty seconds that I drove from one intersection to the next that needed my attention. What if someone was trying to get hold of me? What if I didn't answer an email immediately? It got so bad that I was excited when my two teenagers got their driving permits because it meant that they could drive me around, and I could work while they drove. Talk about a distraction!!

What was actually going on was that I'd created an overwhelming need to constantly fill the empty space in my life. I had an addiction to *doing*. Are you addicted to *doing*? What things distract you from your priorities or goals? Are there certain activities, habits, or people that take up a lot of your time and attention? How do these distractions make you feel, and what impact do they have on your overall sense of well-being and fulfillment?

My mentor taught me to keep a time schedule that includes weekly priorities, weekly meetings, and daily tasks. When I first started using it, I felt overwhelmed by adding something that specific to my plate. Now, thanks to my schedule, I start tasks more efficiently and complete them more effectively. I learned that I was spending way too much time on things that weren't serving me or moving me toward my goals. I was also able to take a step back and see where in my life I could hire someone to take care of those tasks that weren't a good use of my time. It was eye-opening to see it all written down.

Now it's your turn to write an inventory of your time to determine how you spend it. Reflect on your typical weekday and write down a detailed account of how you spend your time, from the moment you wake up until you go to bed. Be honest with yourself and include everything from checking your phone in the morning to watching TV before sleep.

_____

_____

_____

_____

_____

_____

_____

Look at your time inventory and ask yourself, "What am I doing that no longer serves me?" Take a red pen and cross out the things that you can remove from your daily routine that are distracting you. Start with one or two. Don't overwhelm yourself with instant or dramatic change. Remember, distractions actively work against you! Cut them down to allow the gift of presence to come in and create more peace and growth.

Path of Least Resistance

"Take the path of least resistance." You've probably heard this phrase a lot. But what does it really mean? And how do you take it? And, most importantly, is it always the best choice?

There's a difference between taking the path of least resistance and taking the easy way out. When you take the easy way out, it's lazy. You see resistance ahead and decide that you don't want to even try. When you take the easy way out, you miss opportunities to learn and grow. When you take the easy way out, you limit yourself and your potential by trying to avoid difficult situations. If you're alive, you will eventually encounter obstacles, so stop trying to avoid them! Rather, learn how to be adaptable and master whatever lies ahead.

Instead of living in denial and avoiding the uncomfortable, when resistance comes up (and it will), recognize it and ask yourself, "What is this here to teach me?" Be curious. In that moment, you are saying to God, the Universe, your higher power, "I trust you. I know you're guiding me and leading me where I need to go. I know you put this desire into my heart and that you will steer me in the right direction." When you put your trust in the vision, knowing that your desire is pure, you move toward your dreams with ease. That is the path of least resistance! And guess what? It's more fun that way, too! Don't spend so much time focusing on the end result that you don't see anything but the finish line! You won't enjoy the process and the journey! The entire journey *is the point*. It's the whole reason why you reach a goal and immediately look for a new one.

The pursuit of your dreams pushes you to step outside your comfort zone, confront obstacles, and develop resilience and perseverance. It's rare that the path to your dreams will be without obstacles. It will have ups and downs, but, through those experiences, you will grow, learn, and evolve. Each challenge you face and overcome strengthens your character, builds your confidence, and expands your capabilities. Use these moments as opportunities of self-discovery because you may find even more hidden talents, passions, and interests! You will have a deeper understanding of your values, strengths, and areas for improvement. This self-awareness is a powerful tool that shapes not only your pursuit of dreams, but also your overall personal growth and fulfillment.

Going on this journey takes much energy and effort, so be sure to prioritize your self-care through each step, lest you end up burned out. Burnout leads to lack of motivation, lack of fulfillment, and, eventually, deters you from moving forward when things feel hard.

Instead, focus on the consistent renewal of energy that will inspire you to move through the journey with ease and, therefore, help you attract what you need to enjoy the journey. In order to do this, you will need to understand what it means to truly surrender.

Full Surrender

A lot of coaches and healing gurus talk about the power of surrendering. Surrendering fear, control, and anxiety. But when you're caught in fear, control, and anxiety, surrendering doesn't feel like an option. I once worked with a coach who told me to visualize all my fears and anxiety in a box. I had to be very specific, down to the nitty gritty. I then had to take that box and hand it up to God in full surrender. Sounds easy, right? It wasn't. I was a sobbing mess, trying to release control of all of these things to God. I felt like He had better things to worry about.

I'll be honest, I didn't release them during that session. Even though it was a mental exercise, I couldn't "physically" hand it over. But it opened my eyes to all of the things in my life that I believed I had control over, revealing everything that was clouding my energy toward a stress-free, fully-flowing life. I had to get honest with myself about everything in that box that I couldn't release. And, more importantly, why I couldn't release them.

If you can't be honest about your actions, anxieties, and fears, you will continue to be held back by them and enable them to affect the way that everything else flows into your life.

What are your fears and anxieties? Write them out, put them in the box, and hand them over! They don't serve you anymore. I recommend grabbing two pieces of paper and cutting them into eight squares. Then, find a quiet place, preferably one that makes you feel happy and allows you to be open to self-reflection. On each piece of paper, write down, in as much detail as you possibly can, the fears and anxieties you want to remove from your life. Write down what they are, how they make you feel, how they're keeping you from moving forward, and how you're going to shift to a better feeling, thought, or action. Don't be afraid to be detailed, vulnerable, and raw; you will be the only one who looks at these. Next, hold them in your hand all together. Take a deep breath and give gratitude for this moment of change in your life for releasing the things that no longer serve you. Once you've peacefully detached from the energy that these things bring to you, throw them away for good!

Fresh Start

"If you want to become someone else,
you have to become aware of who you are."
-Joe Dispenza

When you are truly able to surrender these fears, doubts, and anxieties, you will make room in your life for new thoughts and activities that will be more aligned with your vision. Each day that you wake up is a new opportunity. Set intentions at the beginning of the day. Who do you want to show up as? Say it out loud and claim it as the "you" you want to be.

If you don't currently practice daily journaling, it's time to start. As a previous journaling avoidant, I'm here to tell you that simply taking five to ten minutes each day to write down my gratitude and intentions for the day has been a game changer for me. Making it intentional has created lasting momentum. Write down at least three to five thoughts that you will stay conscious of throughout the day. Maybe it's who you show up as or how you want to treat people. It could be how you want to pay it forward or be an inspiration to someone else. Next, write out three to four things you want to change in your life or in yourself. Is it how you act? Is it the emotions that you live by? Do you have gratitude or a victim mentality? Is it possible you live with guilt without even realizing?

Now say what thoughts, behaviors, and choices you want to make throughout the day and then practice them. Over time, and with consistency, you will reframe the way your brain automatically opens up and shows up for the world and yourself. Remember the neuroplasticity I wrote about earlier? This is another practice to achieve it! Once you start on that new path and stay consistent with it, your brain will physically create new pathways that will lead you to the new and improved you!

It's also time to start to surrender painful, negative thoughts and feelings and connect to gratitude. Just ten minutes of daily gratitude (including feeling it) increases your immune system function by fifty percent by promoting a sense of calmness and decreasing stress. When you consciously focus on what you're grateful for, whether it's your health, supportive relationships, or the beauty of nature, your body releases hormones that contribute to a more balanced and resilient immune system. Moreover, when you feel grateful, you feel more positive, which, in turn, encourages you to focus on healthy choices like working out and eating better, which also are immune-boosting activities. When you are in a state of gratitude, you have better relationships and social interactions, which give you a sense of belonging. When you feel this way, you again trigger your "feel good" hormones.

Overall, surrendering into gratitude helps you avoid being on autopilot. When you're on autopilot, working from a subconscious level, you lose a sense of presence and joy. It's like that movie with Adam Sandler where he received a magic remote that could fast-forward him through time. It felt so beneficial at the moment to be able to skip through the hard parts and get to the glory. But, instead, anytime he would fast-forward, he would be on autopilot around his loved ones. When he looked back on those times, he noticed that he was not fully present or emotionally available. Because of this, he lost connection with the people that he cared about. When you're not fully present and engaged, you may miss opportunities for self-reflection, exploration, and learning new knowledge or skills. It becomes harder to challenge yourself, step out of your comfort zone, and embrace new experiences.

Also when you're on autopilot, you risk making bad choices. When you're not consciously aware of your actions, decisions, and the impact they have on your life, you may drift away from what truly matters. It can lead to feeling stuck or unsatisfied, as you're not actively steering your life in the direction you desire.

When you don't fully surrender, you're fighting an uphill battle, struggling to hold on to things that are no longer serving you. Holding onto these things drains your limited resources and can discourage you. It's dream crushing, and you aren't here for that.

Fully surrendering is a necessity; it's not an option. It's a powerful tool that helps you release control, which helps you release resistance, which creates true flow. Fully surrendering is not admitting defeat; it's a first step toward victory!

What are you holding onto that you need to release control over? Write it down.

_____

_____

_____

_____

_____

_____

Is this something that you can actively work on releasing? What would your life look like without it? How would it create ease for you?

Surrendering allows you to release control and open up to the natural flow of your desire to manifest into your reality. By surrendering, you tap into a deeper level of intuition and wisdom. In full surrender, you're no longer consumed by fear and anxiety. You're able to tune into your inner guidance system and make decisions from a place of clarity and purpose. It takes a tremendous amount of courage and faith to do this, but the rewards are well worth that effort! When you surrender, you open yourself to a world of possibility that you've never even imagined before!

If you're holding onto something that's causing you pain and frustration, take a deep breath, and commit to surrendering the control you want to possess over it. Let go of that need to control the outcome, and trust that it will work out as it is meant to. You might be surprised at how quickly things start to fall into place once you surrender and ally yourself with the natural flow of your life.

Faith-Based Living

When you face challenges and obstacles in your life, whether it's health issues, financial struggles, or relationship problems, what supports you? For me, it's faith. Faith means different things to different people. For some, faith is a belief in a higher power or divine intervention. I believe in God. But I don't view God as a puppeteer in the sky who chooses who gets to have a good life and who doesn't. Rather, I believe that energy is responsible for life and that God is energy. For others, faith is a sense of trust and confidence in themselves and their ability to overcome challenges.

Whatever your definition might be, there's no denying its power in difficult times. When you have faith, you have hope. When you have faith, you believe that things will get better. It gives you strength and resilience to get through whatever life throws your way. Having faith is a decision that you have the power to make. You can choose good-feeling thoughts or you can choose bad-feeling thoughts. Of course, following God or a higher power does not mean that nothing bad will ever happen to you. Faith does not mean that you won't face challenges or experience pain. It means that you will have the courage and the resilience to face those challenges, learn from them, and allow them to draw you deeper into the meaning of life.

When my youngest son was born at twenty-three weeks gestation, did I have faith? Was I freaking out? Was I scared that I was going to have to plan a funeral for my child? Yes, yes, and an astounding yes! Looking back, it would've been so easy for me to feel hopeless and throw my hands up in the air in defeat. Do you know the survival rate of a baby born that early? Less than one percent. I had every single piece of scientific evidence telling me that my child was not going to make it. I had four doctors tell me four different times that I needed to let him go. They said he would have absolutely no quality of life. He would never walk, talk, be able to feed himself, or even say "I love you." From an outsider's perspective, I pretty much had every "right" to surrender to science and end his life. Why didn't I? Faith. It's one of the best gifts that women have, an ancient intuition. I knew deep within myself that letting him go was not an option. I'm proud to say that now he is fifteen, self-sufficient, can walk, talk, feed himself, and tells me he loves me at least twenty-five times a day!

Maybe this whole faith thing doesn't come easily to you right now. That's okay! What's important is that you are here with a hunger and a passion to see significant change in your life. Throughout this book, you have gained new tools and knowledge to help you with the next steps toward following your dreams and finding your purpose. It's up to you now to implement and grow with what you know! The dream that you have been dreaming is calling you right now. It's calling you in and asking you to say yes! Will you answer that call?

PARTING WORDS

Remember that you have the power within you to create the life that you desire. Embrace this journey of healing and personal growth with an open heart and curious mind. Celebrate your progress, no matter how big or small. Stay connected to your inner wisdom and guidance system that has been there all along. Embrace your uniqueness and surrender the comparison.

You are worthy of love, happiness, and fulfillment!

Every single moment of this journey is a testimony. Though my journey led me through heartaches and fear, it also is what led me to write this book for you.

If I hadn't gone through those experiences, I wouldn't have written this to help you find the courage to move forward toward everything that you desire.

I see you, I hear you, I am you!

Go and change the world like you were meant to.

With love,

Jenna

ABOUT THE AUTHOR

Jenna Griffith is a purpose and prosperity expert, renowned certified compassion coach, and founder of the Service and Soul Group. As a former military wife and current wife of a first responder, she empowers other military and first responder wives to find their purpose and embrace their skills and passions. She firmly believes that military and first responder wives have their own path beyond their role as a spouse, and she strives to support them in realizing their potential, as well as save marriages and strengthen families by fostering their personal growth and self-discovery.

A dedicated advocate, Jenna provides a wealth of resources to help these women navigate their unique challenges while still serving alongside their husbands. Through her courses, workshops, and books, she empowers military and first responder wives to overcome obstacles and answer the questions, "What do I do now?" and "What is my purpose?" She guides them to feel whole as they pursue their own dreams. An empathetic caretaker, Jenna is motivated to share her knowledge and experiences to help other women discover their true calling and equip them with the necessary tools to embark on their own transformative journeys.

Throughout her life, Jenna faced numerous challenges, including being a teenage mother, caring for a micro-preemie baby, and aiding in her ex-husband's recovery from a helicopter accident. With a background in health and healing, she possesses a strong foundation in guiding others toward personal growth and fulfillment.

To connect with Jenna and learn more about her work, please visit serviceandsoul.com.

Made in the USA
Middletown, DE
07 April 2024

52616233R00088